I Wish I Knew This Before My Divorce

I Wish I Knew This Before My Divorce

Ending the Battle Between Holding On and Letting Go

Elaine O. Foster, Ph.D.

Joseph W. Foster

PsyConOps

I Wish I Knew This Before My Divorce

Ending the Battle Between Holding On and Letting Go

Editing by Lisa Baci

Illustrations by Nebojsa Obradovic

Publisher's Note

This publication is designed to provide accurate and authoritative information regarding the subject of divorce. It is sold with the understanding that the publisher is not engaged in rendering psychological, financial, legal, or other professional services. If expert assistance or counseling is needed, the services of a competent professional should be sought.

PsyConOps Publishing

http://www.PsyConOps.com

Library of Congress Cataloging – in – Publication Data

Foster, Elaine O. & Foster, Joseph W.

ISBN-10: 0-9895077-9-3

ISBN-13: 978-0-9895077-9-0

Published by PsyConOps Publishing

Printed in the United States of America

Contents

Acknowledgements

To the gentle readers of our first book, *In Movement There Is Peace*.

You gave us the courage to try our hand at a topic that we both struggled with for years, building happiness after divorce. Writing this book as a couple created tensions that surprised and tortured us to the very last page. The final product has been tested, empirically and in the equally important school of hard knocks.

Many thanks go out to the friends and associates that provided constructive feedback and editing of this book. Their many hours of work helped make this book a success.

~ EOF and JWF

To my parents, Winslow and Lydia,

for teaching me the importance of love in the face of adversity.

Going through my divorce, a first for our family, could have blotted out other firsts, like getting a doctorate and being commissioned as an officer in the Air Force, but you stood by me for all of it. Sharing lessons of healing for those who know divorce pain is my humble way of paying your love forward.

And to my family:

Joe, who helps me spackle over the cracks of my relationship fears,
our son, Ben, for teaching me to take chances and to stretch my legs out far enough to land on my feet,
our son, Andrew, for reminding me I can still cry over little things,
our daughter, Makenna, for showing me how to forgive and live.
This book is a reflection of the courage they taught me by example. ~ EOF

Elaine and I are opposites in the way that our reflections in a mirror are opposites of our true image. This book wouldn't have happened without her stubborn dedication and unwavering drive to help others who are experiencing the same tragedy we'd both experienced. I, on the other hand, am not all that altruistic and needed constant prodding along the way. My nature is to live in the moment: unencumbered by plans, deadlines and self-imposed responsibilities. Terrible characteristics for writing a book. Together, Elaine and I reach a balance that values both approaches, that reflects both approaches: to divorce, to writing, and to life. Thanks, Darling. ~ JWF

Introduction

Chances are you've opened this book because you're trying to solve a problem, the problem called divorce. You struggle for the right solution: be more loving, stay patient, find a marriage therapist. When that fails, you consider dropping the carrot and grabbing the stick. Maybe you threaten to take something valuable-- the kids, the dog, the home computer. Money can scare people too: “I'll take every penny you've got!” Good cop, bad cop —none of these strategies seem to work. You want to hold tight, but your marriage keeps slipping away like a loose wedding band.

Your spouse has already found their fix. They're working on a new plan and their solution is just a lawyer away. You're in a face-off of irreconcilable differences. But here's the kicker: the two of you want the same thing. What's that? You both want the pain go away. Your solution is to stay together; their solution is to break apart.

It's easy to sink deep into the problem of divorce because we start with a universal premise: divorce is bad. It's a mirror of our failure ... of failed decisions, failed family, failed love. Gone is that secure feeling of knowing “who loves ya baby?” You feel as if the person that had your back is stabbing you right between the shoulder blades. How can two intelligent people hold such opposing solutions to a mutual problem? And what is the best solution: staying together or breaking apart?

Who This Book Is For

When my husband, Joe, and I wrote the first draft of this book, our editor asked a simple question, “Is this book for people who are trying to save their marriage or for the ones who want to recover from a divorce?" She asked because most people searching for a divorce book fall into those two categories.

"This book isn't for either," I explained.

She did not look happy. Yes, editors improve grammar, but the good ones also edit for a target audience. "There is no divorce help category called 'neither,'" she advised with more than a hint of irritation. "People want to know how you're going to help them fix their problem."

"But that's exactly why we're writing this book," Joe said. "To show readers that they don't have to be forced down a path before they've had a chance to climb the mountain to get a better view of the terrain."

We wrote this book for people who are willing to explore before seeking solutions to the dilemma of a departing spouse. It's a guide for the mindful: for those who are willing to peer at the picture on the puzzle box before grabbing at pieces. There are plenty of books out there on how to fight for your marriage, and even more texts on how to let go and survive after being left. They treat divorce like emotional bypass surgery for the brokenhearted. This book is different. It uses principles from the "third wave" of cognitive-behavioral therapy to help those in the early stages of divorce to find their joy, in or out of marriage. It's the companion Joe and I wish existed when we were going through our separate walks-of-fire ten years ago.

Before my breakup I was serving in the Air Force, working 60 hours a week and feeling overwhelmed. When my ex-husband moved out, I told myself I had two paths to choose from: either fight for my marriage or walk away. It wasn't hard for me to decide. I knew I wanted to save my relationship, and like Winston Churchill, my plan was to "Never give up!" That path of resistance ended in a divorce that tore my seven years of marriage asunder. I spent a lot of time suffering and second-guessing what else I could have done to save my marriage. For years, I wracked my brain wondering why I wasn't able to stop the divorce. Worse yet, all that self-blame clouded my vision for the new life that was waiting for me. Despite a thriving career in the military as a clinical psychologist, I felt like a failure—ashamed and unloved. I could see no path out of suffering.

Avoiding the Pain

What have you tried so far to stop your divorce? Check all that apply.

- ☐ Asked or begged for a second chance
- ☑ Pushed for marital counseling
- ☐ Looked for the most threatening lawyer available
- ☐ Talked to your spouse's family to help convince your spouse to stay
- ☐ Blocked all communication with your spouse
- ☐ Used alcohol or drugs to numb the pain
- ☐ Threatened to take full custody or limit time with the children
- ☐ Called, emailed, or texted repeatedly to stay in contact
- ☐ Talked to your friends about how awful your spouse is treating you
- ☐ Designed a plan for getting your spouse to change their mind
- ☐ Cursed or blamed your spouse for hurting you or for not trying harder
- ☐ Dated or flirted with someone new
- ☐ Stayed in bed, binge watching or binge eating for comfort
- ☐ Spied on your spouse to see if they're with a lover

If you've checked off more than a couple of these approach-avoidance strategies, don't beat yourself up. They made it on the list because most people try at least one of them. But, like most, you've probably noticed that these diversions haven't stopped the suffering. This book relies on strategies that have helped all kinds of people to live a full and free life, regardless of where their pain is coming from: be it divorce, anxiety, depression, or illness.

What Can I Expect to Learn from This Book?

This book is organized into two sections. In Section I, we'll deconstruct your marriage, searching for the clues that brought you to this point in your life. You'll learn seven common myths about divorce and you'll use this knowledge to better understand how you're feeling, how your spouse might be feeling, and what makes relationships thrive or die. Seeing the way these fictions can block your progress will assist you when it comes time to take committed action.

In the first part of this book, we'll also be guiding you through a marital autopsy. As a type of post-mortem procedure, the autopsy will help you determine exactly why your relationship faltered. Don't let the dissection of your marriage scare you; by the time we get to it, you'll have met a great cast of characters to act as your support system, especially Dan, a man in his late thirties, facing an unwanted divorce. You'll have a chance to watch his reactions through all the rejection and loss of his marriage. We chose Dan's story as the first tool to unpack because he is a type of "everyman" in the struggle through divorce. If you allow him, Dan will place a caring hand on your shoulder and remind you that you're not alone, even when you're feeling totally abandoned. Throughout this section, we'll also take you on a journey using fables, riddles, and real-life cases to help you imagine the new world waiting for you. Before this section ends, you'll read about the common profiles seen in divorce initiators, the spouses we refer to as "Leavers" because they have chosen to walk away. Equal time is devoted to understanding your own divorce grief, and how it differs from the grief of death.

In Section II, you're going to forge a unique path, one that is all your own. There is a middle way you can follow when standing at a fork in the road, if you're willing to explore the landscape. You'll be taking a seven-day journey where you can expect to encounter unfamiliar terrain. It will be hard going at times. You may be tempted to turn back and give up the quest, but when you get that urge, take a deep breath… and relax. By then, you'll have enough tools in your bag to help you find your way. They will allow you to tap into your assumptions about committed relationships and guide you in creating strategies for your future.

Getting the Most Out of This Book

I Wish I Knew This Before My Divorce is more than a book, it's a companion, with exercises created from decades of clinical experience using a distinctive approach known as Acceptance and Commitment Therapy or ACT (pronounced like the word "act"). ACT takes principles from Western psychology and medicine, and turns them upside down. The strategy does not seek to destroy disease or to eliminate symptoms, and yet the people who use it feel better. It combines the logic of science with the soul of Eastern philosophy, focusing on principles like values, compassion, acceptance, and willingness (Hayes, Strosahl and Wilson 2016). The result is a treatment that lifts us beyond our transient thoughts and feelings, to access our unblemished selves. ACT has been tested and proven successful with all kinds of conditions including depression, obsessive-compulsive disorders, chronic pain, stress from terminal cancer, anxiety, posttraumatic stress disorder, anorexia, heroin abuse, and even psychotic spectrum disorders like schizophrenia.

When Joe and I started using ACT and mindfulness strategies in our divorce groups, we knew we had a perfect match. ACT allowed us to meet each person where they stood, lost in pain and suffering, without judging them for their inability "to get over it." This non-judgmental approach will help you grow stronger during a time when you're filled with doubt. We've assembled each exercise in this book to keep you moving at a steady pace. The methods will require practice, even when your emotions feel out of control—especially when your emotions feel out of control. It takes strength to get through the pain of hearing your once-trusted partner say, "I've found someone else," or scream out, "I hate you!" The important thing is, you won't have to do it alone and the chapter on "Leaver" profiles will help you understand some of the motivations behind those words of rejection.

Throughout the chapters, you'll read about people facing separation and divorce. Look closely. We've made sure to sprinkle seeds of wisdom along the path. Each chapter begins with a quote from someone who could be you, someone learning to thrive in the face of divorce.

Take Time for Each Exercise

There is a purpose behind each question and each practice. There will be times when you'll want to skip an exercise. Unless you have a good reason, don't give in to the temptation because you may be avoiding a particular problem. We all have a tendency to put off things that cut close to home. We avoid making phone calls to the dentist, creating a budget, or eating healthy because they brings things into focus that we don't feel ready to address. Pushing yourself through the hard challenges will help you to grow. Of course, if a question doesn't fit your situation, then please, go ahead and skip it. Do what's right for you.

Commit to Turning Off the TV or Computer

Reading is hard when your mind is racing or exhausted from worry. We made our stories relevant and enlightening so that this book can be your devoted coach. Make time to engage with it. A show on TV may entertain, but you're looking for a better life and you won't get that through distraction. Commit to reading at least 30 minutes every day and you'll soon build clarity and purpose.

Give Yourself the Time to Do It Right

This isn't a novel you read from start to finish in one night. Find a place for it on your bed stand, on the floor by your air mattress, or in the bag you carry to work. This is a guide to help you exercise your way through this breakup. Like a fish who's been scooped out of the water, you may be gasping for air and looking for the nearest pond, but instant solutions don't lead to long-lasting growth. Take your time. Some insights do come in a flash, but most of the progress will take time to learn and practice. Be patient. Avoid reading more than a chapter or two at a time so you can incorporate each lesson in a meaningful way.

We Don't Have a Problem Remembering

You'll notice some concepts being repeated several times throughout our book, such as the idea that no person can belong to another. There is a reason for this repetition, it's a deliberate attempt to underscore the guidance that will help you travel the greatest distance. Think of these replays as a type of mind conditioner where the directions advise you to "rinse and repeat" for better results. Retracing allows the lessons to become more familiar, and as such, are intended to help you withstand some of the social indoctrination that can interfere with your new learning. For instance, you may agree in theory that no human being can belong to another, but then you might turn on the radio and hear a song insisting: "You Belong to Me" performed by Patsy Cline, Bing Crosby, Annie Lennox, Carly Simon, Jo Stafford, Taylor Swift… you get the idea. There's a lot of cultural noise to fight against. Repeating the truth is the best way we know to dilute the flood of counter-messages you'll hear throughout your day.

Consider Sharing this Book with Your Therapist or Doctor

If you're in psychotherapy or taking medications for depression or anxiety, consider discussing the use of this book with your therapist. The ACT principles we'll be using are a form of cognitive-behavioral treatment known to many psychologists, clinical social workers and mental health counselors. It's an empirically-supported treatment, meaning there's lots of research to support its effectiveness. If you're seeing a psychiatrist, explain that this book can be an "augmentation strategy" for your antidepressant or anti-anxiety medicine. Most psychiatrists use medicines to help with somatic symptoms like fatigue, insomnia, and concentration. Unfortunately, their patients can continue to struggle with the psychological symptoms of sadness, helplessness, and hopelessness. Using this book as a catalyst for therapy can improve your peace of mind and offer a welcome addition to many therapies.

Why Did A Married Couple Write a Divorce Book?

Joe and I wrote this book because we've experienced divorce firsthand. It's not a concept to us; heartbreak has colored our past and remains our teacher. I met Joe after taking a year off from all romantic relationships. I'd convinced myself I was missing some important relationship gene that gets doled out at conception. For me, another marriage was like stuffing a loaf of bread in a Ziploc sandwich bag, too much effort for crumby results. Joe was the opposite. He used his Nichiren Shoshu Buddhist practices he'd studied as a teenager to explore relationships. By seeing the world as a place for enlightenment, he witnessed powerful changes during a time most adolescents are struggling with shyness and acne. Through daily practices spanning decades, he accepted the fact that his needs would be met if he welcomed all of life's weather patterns instead of cursing the sky for clouds and rain. After our divorces, we met and decided to take a chance; Joe, when he was ready to dedicate himself to a new relationship, and me, when I decided not to give up on love.

They say that opposites attract. Joe's an engineer helping our military warriors train for battle. I help those same warriors recover from the ravages of battle. And the trauma didn't end with them; it bled into their marriages. Despite our mismatched careers and tolerance for commitment, it turned out we had a lot in common. It was a case of Western medicine meets Eastern philosophy and the synergy it sparked took us places we would never have reached alone.

We combined our dialectical training and diversity of experience to start divorce groups at our local military bases—teaching members to look beyond their stories of infidelity and betrayal in order to engage in mindfulness-based practices. This approach revealed truths about the unpredictability of life and relationships. The critical elements of the ACT principals that have transformed people's include:

- ☯ Questioning the words your mind tells you
- ☯ Building patience for the unknown
- ☯ Refraining from judgements about painful events

The results were so dramatic we decided to write a book about the most rewarding

ACT-ions you can take during divorce. Joe used his Buddhist training to tweak the questions and practices you'll read about, but the roots of many of their origins can be found in ACT manuals for therapists. I brought my 25-plus years of clinical experience and case studies to the narrative. The result is a book filled with understanding for your pain. Together, we pulled out all the stops to address the many struggles that happen when a person loses their partner.

You might be surprised to learn that writing this book took a toll on our marriage. It seems the topic of divorce in and of itself has the power to produce tension and conflict, even between two normally compassionate people. There were times we wanted to quit out of fear that the book was taking on a sinister life, stealing our faith in marriage. I admit to setting it aside and taking longer than I'd intended to finish it, but there was always one thing that drove me back to the manuscript—the knowledge that we could help more people than I could ever reach in private practice. We hope that our good intention finds you during your time of struggle and takes you to the places you were meant to discover.

A Note of Caution

In the early stages of separation and divorce, it is not uncommon for emotion-packed exchanges to become physical. Your spouse may feel desperate. You may feel desperate. Most likely you'll have conflicting agendas. What should you do if, over the course of a breakup, two reasonably healthy people engage in acts of aggression? This is a tough call that you're going to have to make based on your history and current safety. Was it completely out of character for your spouse to push you out of the way as they headed for the door? Were you shocked by your own behavior when you put your fist through the dining room wall in rage?

If you find yourself getting wrapped up in toxic blow-ups, there's only one thing to do: disengage. It's dangerous behavior and only makes resentments worse and harder to repair.

Even if your altercations are verbal and have not become physical, it's urgent to call a time out. Think of it as a meaningful opportunity to reflect on your actions and to prevent more destruction. There is a Chinese proverb that warns, "Words are like water, they cannot be un-poured." You might feel a need to lash out, but wait until you're alone. You can cry, call a friend, scream, or kick the trash can across the kitchen, just wait until they're gone.

Without a doubt, if you have been living in an abusive relationship, it needs to be addressed. You know it, and most likely, the people around you know it. Don't let violence become your new (or old) normal. Help is available, please get it and use it. You'll find resources for domestic violence at the end of this book.

Finally, this book is meant to be a self-help tool. It is not a substitute for psychological treatment. The Appendix will guide you if you're wondering about when to get professional help, especially if you're considering medications.

Chapter 1. When is a Problem Not a Problem?

"My wife kept telling me our marriage was over. It was over for her, not for me." James L., air traffic controller

You are about to start a journey. This quest will take you to a new land where you can feel confident and whole despite your grief. The terrain will seem unfamiliar as you take your first steps, but after a few paces, you'll notice how easy it becomes to find your balance. You've always known this remarkable place was out there; the problem was, you had a fuzzy map with no clear directions for getting there. Can you get to this better place by working harder to save your marriage, redoubling your efforts to win your spouse back? It's hard to tell what will work and what might backfire. Let's consider that the way to your new destination won't come from packing better persuasion skills or pointing your flashlight into the past or future. The best option for now is to take a look at where you stand. Let's start by checking out the landscape.

You and your spouse have been walking down a paved path. You had walked this path together just like every other married couple who has followed this same path expecting marriage to last for life. For the most part, you've enjoyed the experience. Sure, there were some rough patches, some muddy spots, and places where the path all but disappeared. The obstacles may have slowed you down, but you still had your partner to make it work. Today's walk feels different. Your spouse has led you down an unfamiliar route along a hard, dusty path, far from your home, with no street signs. As the two of you round a bend in the road, you see that it leads to a distant mountain. From where you stand it doesn't seem insurmountable so you shrug it off. But as you draw closer, the steep slope grows massive and foreboding. You notice black clouds and flashes of lightening up near the peak. A cold wind blows and a chill reaches down to your toes. Something is wrong. You can feel this bad thing coming, but can't figure out what exactly is causing your worry. You take hold of your spouse's hand and walk on. When the two of you reach the foot of the mountain, you see that the path splits; one road heads off to the east, the other to the west, each taking you around the mountain. Your spouse sees it, too, nodding as if they knew this was coming.

Pointing off to the west, they say, "I'm going this way." They drop your hand.

The statement is confusing. Why would they use the word "I'm" when the two of you are walking together?

You start to follow, saying, "What do you mean? We're both going, right?"

Your spouse stops and turns back to face you.

"No, we're not."

You watch in shock as they turn and walk away.

"Where are you going? What's happening?"

Your words sink into the earth unheeded. Your spouse ignores your calls and continues down their path.

A thunderclap shakes the ground and the rain starts pouring. By the time you reach the cover of some trees, you're soaking wet, cold, and alone. You've been left at this fork in the road with two directions to choose from. One follows after your spouse, the other heads off in the opposite direction. As your mind races for answers, you spot a third path, a narrow foot trail heading right up that huge mountain. It doesn't look like an easy stroll, but you see a sign post that rouses your courage:

THE MOUNTAINS YOU ARE CARRYING,
YOU WERE ONLY SUPPOSED TO CLIMB

You take your first shaky steps. Walking deeper into the gloom, you find a high stone wall towering up ahead. At the base is a rampart, with an ancient wooden door, its hinges rusted. As you step toward the door, the ground opens up beneath your feet and you fall into a hole that had been covered with leaves. A trap! The door squeaks open and an old troll pokes his head out of the doorway. He tosses a shovel down into the hole, turns away, then closes and latches the door behind him.

You shout out, "Help!"

No response. Feeling panicky, you look down.

"What am I supposed to do with this shovel?"

Imagine trying to get out of a hole by digging at the ground beneath you. No matter how much energy you put into digging, the shovel only adds distance between you and the surface. Maybe you can't see the solution because of your preconceptions of how a shovel is supposed to be used. You're following an age-old tradition of digging down into the dirt. Does it make sense to keep digging if you're already in a hole?

While pondering your predicament, you hear the door unlatch and creak open again. The troll steps to the edge of the pit and stares down at you, his nostrils flaring so wide you can see the frizzy nose hairs behind his furry whiskers.

He asks, "When is a hole not a hole?"

You yell, "I have no clue. Get me out of here!"

"Then thou shalt not pass from this gloom." His dry lips curl into a smirk as he seems to take glee over your turmoil.

It's hard to think but still you try. "Hole...not a hole? What the hell! I'm surrounded by dirt and darkness. I'm too far down to pull myself out. This is a freaking hole, damn it!"

The troll kicks a clump of damp soil onto your head and closes the door again. You hear him cackling with delight from the other side as the bolt slides shut.

You mumble some more, but this time you stop and take a good look around. Concentrate! "What if the hole isn't a problem? What if it's a puzzle?"

The troll, the wall and the locked door are metaphors for the psychic barriers that are keeping you from finding a solution to your problem. These obstacles are blocking your path to a higher ground where you can get a better view of your surroundings.

How would you solve this puzzle? By getting angry and stamping your feet? By panicking out of a fear of suffocating under the packed earth surrounding you? By calling out for your spouse? Those are normal first reactions, but something more needs to happen. You have to open your eyes and take a good look around. To solve a riddle, you must be willing to detach from your assumptions. Look for alternatives. Stay curious.

Try this mental exercise: Put down your shovel and take a deep, slow breath. Release your fear and frustration long enough to see what's around you. You see dirt. You see your shovel. How might you move forward? You could try digging some stairs to climb your way out but you still wouldn't be able to get past the locked door and the troll. The answer comes to you in a stroke of fear turned inside out.

Several hours later, the troll bends over a lamb roasting on a fire. Drool dribbles from the creases in his mouth, falling onto the meat in rivulets of saliva. He's startled by something moving out of the corner of his eye. He turns and squints in the direction of the door.

"It is you!" he exclaims. "You freed yourself without my permission."

You see the shock on his face and, for a moment, you've forgotten how sad and abandoned you were feeling.

With a huff of pride, you call out, "A hole is not a hole when it's a tunnel!"

The troll looks at you now with new appreciation. He motions you to the spit, slicing off a piece of mutton as a lure, catching it with his grimy fingers before it can plunge back into the fire.

"No thanks, I'm not hungry," you say.

There's no way you're going near him now that you're back on the path. But you're trying to stay friendly, just in case he's got some other tricks up his tattered sleeve. He gnaws at a mutton shank with black, jagged teeth. The image makes you queasy, so you turn to scope out the trees ahead.

"Before you go, you must answer one more riddle," he says. "Answer me true and I will gift you a map of the treacherous forest ahead."

Treacherous forest? Map? By now you're certain that those trees are an allegory for the deeper, greater challenges ahead. Okay you decide, it's probably worth a little more time to get proper directions. Plus, you're feeling confident about your big win.

The hunchbacked troll leaves his meal to join you on the path. You figured out the hole, but he knows this next one will really stump you. He starts with a whisper, his breath so rancid you can barely hold still as he presses his lips to your ear, "When is a problem, not a problem?"

Riddles, paradoxes, unexpected twists; we enjoy them in fairy tales, not so much in our relationships. We see life through a lens. Sometimes it's cloudy, sometimes concave so that we can only see short distances and fall into traps based on our assumptions. This book is a companion for your mind, your greatest tool, far more powerful than any shovel. Your logical mind has a natural tendency to seek out solutions when faced with problems that seem insurmountable; in this case, the riddle is your divorce.

The tools you will take on this journey are extracted from principles forged by pioneers in the field of psychology: Therapists like Milton Erikson, famous for his work using the power of suggestion and heightened forms of consciousness. Thought leaders with swirls of artistry like Elizabeth Kübler Ross, Victor Frankl and Kahlil Gibran. And of course, visionaries like Jon Kabat-Zinn and Steven Hayes who employ ACT and mindfulness for all types of problems, from chronic pain to anxiety. Both ACT and Eriksonian theory rely heavily on stories and metaphors to speak to the creative mind. Stories are powerful because they rely on a core truth: humans use universal experiences to solve problems. Think back to archetypal stories about love lost, like Romeo and Juliet, or of paradise lost, like Adam and Eve. Notice how these tales create threads that bind our human experience. Each story contains forgotten lessons that echo within what psychiatrist Carl Jung called our *collective unconscious*, the part of our mind that carries the memories of our ancestors, not just our personal history.

The troll speaks to the part of your brain that can suspend belief in order to engage your hidden, ancestral wisdom. Your logical mind knows this fantastical creature doesn't exist, and yet, you can picture him looking down on you, spraying you with spittle as he shouts his commands. Our dreams do the same thing; they drop us into places where we can fly, fall off cliffs, or swim like a dolphin. Many of our fantasies, dreams, or nightmares could never happen in real life, but that doesn't stop our unconscious from weaving a believable tapestry out of unlikely events.

Don't let the word unconscious scare you. Milton Erikson said, "If I read something that inspires me, my unconscious mind has been changed." The unconscious mind plays a critical role in all of our mental activity. Right now you're probably sitting or lying down with this book. Because you're focused on the words and their meaning, you probably aren't aware of the sensation of the chair or mattress against your back. Now that I've mentioned it, you can feel pressure as you continue resting, but a moment ago you didn't. Our unconscious mind stores all kinds of data that get sent to the brain's back burner, mostly because they are in the past, are already habit (as in muscle memory), or are just not necessary for immediate survival.

Think about the unconscious as the basement of a house, there's a lot of stuff down there, but in order to grab something specific, like your boots, you need to turn on the light and go down the stairs. The tools in this book will introduce you to people and stories designed to focus the light in strategic ways. The stories will tug at your forgotten learnings—wisdom from past generations, from your childhood, or before your marriage—lessons that you forgot you knew. The troll, the allegories, and the real-life stories you will read in this book are designed to show you that people and situations are not always what they seem. Life is rarely predictable. Despite our beliefs about how things should go, we can only take a singular path. We discover that life can be smarter than our plans.

Is it possible to help the process along so that we recognize when life is presenting us with a better plan? The answer is "Yes." With focused attention, we can speak to our unconscious fears and limitations so that our behaviors become more hopeful and realistic, no matter what obstacles we encounter along the way. The ability to accept unhappy events without struggle gives you the power to turn problems into serendipity—a problem is no longer a problem but rather a fortunate turn of events. Releasing the strife doesn't mean passively accepting every dismal thing that happens to you. Doing that would only lead to helplessness and rob you of self-determination. But it does mean staying open long enough to determine what is and is not real, and what is and is not under your control.

When is a problem not a problem?

This riddle takes some mental stretching. Don't be afraid of wrong answers. Fear will only cloud your vision and stifle exploration. For the moment, let the fear float away like smoke from the troll's roasting pit.

As you stand on the path, conjuring about answers, a dog walks by. The pooch sniffs at the air and makes a beeline for the juicy mutton shank by the fire. The troll, who'd been spying the stray, makes a dive for the mutton, reaching it at the very same moment as the dog. For the next few seconds, the two are locked in a tug of war—the troll pulling, the dog resisting; the dog pulling, the troll resisting. Suddenly, the dog lets go and the troll falls to the ground, holding fast to his mutton shank. You look at his fat, heaving belly shining with mutton grease as the dog scampers off with the carcass that had been hanging, unguarded, over the pit.

You smack your forehead in a flash of understanding and wave goodbye.

"Thanks, but I can do this without your map."

The troll lifts himself off the ground. He's so enraged, he throws the hard-won meat onto the dirt.

"Impossible! You'll get lost!"

"Getting lost is just an excuse to explore," you reply.

The sun is peaking out through the clouds now. You pull your sunglasses out of your pocket to shield your eyes from the daylight. A wave of calm washes over your body. You gauge the sun's position in order to set your direction and begin walking toward the woods.

The troll is seething. He follows close behind, bobbing with fury, stamping dirt clouds with his grimy sandals.

"Explore? Without food and water?" he asks. "You won't last a day!"

"There's lots of stuff to eat in the forest. Animals do it all the time."

You feel a tug at your shirttail and look over your shoulder to see the poor creature panting with exhaustion.

"Wait!" The troll looks haggard now as he digs for something under a rock. It's a worn, leather satchel.

"What do you want now?" You're curious but feign annoyance.

"You are a sly one," he says as he opens the bag and pulls out a wrinkled, hand drawn map. "You've solved the riddle."

"I don't know what you're talking about." You really do, because it was so easy to figure out once you saw what happened with the dog.

The troll says, "A problem is not a problem..."

You finish his sentence,"...when there's no struggle."

He hands you the map with his gnarled fingers.

"Take it. You have earned this."

He scratches his whiskers for a moment. Reaching out his hands, he offers you the satchel with a penitent smile.

"In fact, take the whole bag with you."

He looks different, kind of warm and caring, like the Grinch after his heart grew three sizes in the Dr. Seuss story.

He looks into your eyes and says, "Take it as my gift, for I see goodness in you. I do believe you deserve this kindness."

You reach for the troll's hand and he steps forward to hug you.

"One last riddle," he says. "But this one comes with the answer."

You wait politely since he's being extra nice.

"How do you make God laugh?" He pauses for a moment, searching for your expression.

You've heard this one before.

"Plan your future," the two of you say in unison.

Your unexpected synchrony tickles the troll so much, his laughter follows you into the forest.

Chapter One Lessons:

- Being lost is an excuse to explore
- You don't need anyone's permission to take control of your life
- Life can turn out better than your original plans
- When you stop struggling against a problem, you build energy for creating solutions

Chapter 2. The Change You Resist Persists

"She humiliated me. But I kept moving forward, not far, just forward." Dan B., mechanical engineer.

A picture is worth a thousand words and stories create moving pictures in our minds. Before people learned to write, they gathered around the fire sharing tales passed down from generation to generation in oral tradition. Allegories and fables help therapists and ministers to offer lessons without sounding preachy. Do you remember your favorite stories as a child? How many ended with these familiar words: "And the moral of the story is… " A moral satisfies. It's that spray of whipped cream over the banana split. When the hare in Aesop's fable learns a virtue, like "slow but steady wins the race," we learn vicariously by imagining ourselves in the same situation. The tortoise gives us permission to take our time, knowing that things will work out if we stay focused and take determined steps. We don't have to run the race to take the lesson; our brain gives us the capacity to learn by watching what the tortoise does to win and why the hare loses in the end. But, there is a dark side to believing the language of these stories and the language of our mind. They tell us to think that "they all lived happily ever after," creating an expectation that there would be no more pitfalls along the way.

Beyond cautionary tales, stories capture our interest in ways that lectures can't. We may get distracted during a webinar, but, like rubberneckers on the highway, we snap to attention when the instructor tells about how he hit a car on the way to class. Stories with emotion, stories with suspense, narrow escapes and near fatalities capture our interest because they tap into a universal habit to compare our lives to others, to wonder what happens next.

Your satchel holds tools designed to teach, caution, and inspire. It contains Dan's story, a type of Swiss Army knife we will use for opening, carving, peeling, and tightening your understanding of divorce. Dan's breakup was real, and so was his struggle. As you continue your journey, his actions and reactions will act like a camera, taking close-ups and long shots of the rocky terrain called "detachment." Use his experience for guidance; like the tortoise, allow him to inspire you by observing his progress. Compare your thoughts and actions to his. Try to imagine what he will do next or just think about what you would do in his situation.

Dan's Story

It was a Thursday night at the local United Methodist Church. Joe and I arrived a half-hour early to set up the seats for our *Paths of Divorce* group. Dan was the first person to show up. He looked homeless. His clothes were rumpled and his chin glistened with salt-n-pepper stubble. He looked like he hadn't slept in days.

I approached him and asked, "Are you here for the divorce group?"

He reached out his hand to shake mine, and I noticed his fingernails were bitten down to the nub.

"Yeah. I'm Dan. A friend of mine told me I should come to your group. He said it helped."

"That's good to hear," I said, sliding a chair out and taking a seat to face him. He had arrived before the other group members so it gave us some time and a brief bit of privacy.

"Are you okay sharing about your divorce?" I asked.

"I'm not divorced. At least not yet."

Dan explained that his wife had moved out with their children a month earlier. He was thirty-nine and worked for the past thirteen years as an Air Force civil engineer. He'd been married to Leigh for seven years, and they had two daughters in grade school. We were just getting to his living arrangements when the other group members started trickling in. Dan responded to each person with a short nod but said nothing. I assumed he was uncomfortable with strangers, like so many of the people who attend a group for the first time. His silence melted away when it was his turn to check in. He took the floor like a pro.

"Hi, I'm Dan. My wife left me a month ago and…"

After ten minutes of talking I interrupted Dan to rein him back into the give and take of the group session.

I asked, "Dan, what do you want to get out of coming to group?"

He wasn't ready to stop. This need to review the shock and betrayal of divorce is so common that it goes by various names: verbal incontinence, circumstantial speech, or what some have less affectionately called "verbal diarrhea."

After fifteen years of leading divorce groups, I've separated the verbal incontinence of divorce into two categories, acute and chronic.

Verbal Incontinence of Divorce

*** Acute**
These individuals are early in the breakup and are trying to work through their spouse's decision to leave. They can't believe what's happening. Like a car that has suddenly lost traction in the rain, their words reflect a kind of mental tailspin. The need to talk excessively about the divorce is a type of overcorrection for the loss of control they are feeling. For acute sufferers, the excessive need to process the divorce experience resolves naturally over time, either spontaneously or with the help of supportive relationships.

*** Chronic**
These individuals remain stuck in shock and dismay. Although their divorce took place years ago, they can't accept it. People in this category are like clay that has stiffened over time. They show minimal malleability and little momentum for change. Some continue to soliloquize about their divorce even when they are in a new relationship. Their friends have often stopped listening because the tune doesn't change. There's a vicious cycle going on here: the encouragement from friends and family dwindles because it seems to make no difference. The withdrawal by friends or family leads to greater hopelessness in the victim and more skips on the scratched record. Progress is still possible, but it usually requires professional help to break through the mental grooves caused by their suffering.

Dan continued, "Losing Leigh was like a punch to the gut. No matter how hard I try, I can't stop thinking about her. I can't sleep. I can't eat. I've lost twelve pounds. It takes everything I've got just to make it to work every day. I had to leave early yesterday. I just couldn't pull it together. I feel stuck. My friends tell me to move on, but I can't. I just can't."

"Dan, you're having a normal reaction," I offered.

"I don't wanna hear that! I hear that all the time. "

Dan was the lion in Aesop's fable, batting at anyone drawing near--even a doctor approaching to examine the thorn in his paw.

"Nothing is normal anymore. My family is gone. My wife, my girls. My girls are my life." He pressed the heels of his palms against his downturned forehead, as if trying to squash his thoughts.

"She told me she doesn't love me anymore. My life is over. I know it. She says she's going to take half my retirement and the house. She's moved on but I can't. I know I just need to sign the freaking divorce papers and get it over with, but they just sit there on the counter with the rest of my mail."

Group members exchanged knowing expressions. They'd all been in that same dark place, where the simple act of opening an envelope feels like you're prying an alligator's teeth apart.

"It's tempting to get it over with just to stop the pain," Joe said. "And anger is a frequent feeling during divorce, when everything that matters is ripped away in a one-sided decision, a decision with no invitation for discussion. You want your wife back. You want the pain to go away. How to make that happen is where you get stuck."

"I'm so pissed off over all this, I can't stand it."

Joe nodded and said, "We men are more inclined to cut our ties because we experience our feelings as overwhelming. We also lack social support for expressing our emotions, having learned early that 'big boys don't cry.' So we toss our feelings into a blender; pouring in sadness and grief and shame and guilt. A few pulses later, we pour out one very potent feeling ... anger. And anger scares people away, especially when we act it out instead of feel it out."

"I don't want to lose my family." Dan replied. "Even though I already have."

Joe asked. "Would you be willing to hang on for a little while longer before signing the papers?"

Joe knew that holding on was exactly what he wanted. Dan was waiting and praying for a miracle to save his marriage.

"I can hang on. I love my family."

~

Does Dan's situation sound familiar? Are you feeling betrayed, confused, unloved, angry, depressed? Maybe, like Dan, those feelings can be wrapped up in one all-encompassing word—pain. Joe's comments spoke to gender differences that exist in the male and female response to the pain of divorce.

Gender Reactions to Pain and Suffering

Ron Levant, former president of the American Psychological Association (APA), publicized the struggle men have with their feelings. He used the term "normative male alexithymia" (alexithymia literally means, "having no words for emotions") to explain the phenomenon, observing that men have difficulty identifying and expressing vulnerable emotions such as despair, sadness, and fear (Levant 2001).

Women don't tend to show the same struggle with alexithymia. Because of the social support they receive for sharing their emotions, they can typically tease out different feelings when a relationship ends. For women, the challenge is not the inability to label feelings, it's the emotions they do claim during divorce. They often own more than their share of shame, guilt, and helplessness. Because women are socialized to value and nurture relationships, being left by a partner sends a weighty message that they failed to build consensus. According to Deborah Tannen, author of the book, *You Just Don't Understand*, women value community. The tribe offers understanding and support. Females buy ice cream, pour wine, and come equipped with a box of tissues for a good cry. All of it "acknowledges the pain." This acceptance of vulnerability may be the reason why women have an advantage over men, mentally and physically, outside of marriage. It may also be why women tend to seek divorce more often than men. The greater support available for women may act as a buffer against the unknown in a way that is less available to men in our culture. Also, gender inequality in marriage persists, making it more likely for women to feel less fulfilled in marriage than men.

Of course, there are many individual differences and these observations don't apply in all cases. Many women identify with rage more than any other emotion, and many men stuck it out longer than some women facing divorce. Either way, there are important distinctions between men and women that influence their actions and reactions during a separation.

We were close to the end of our group session when I moved to wrap things up.

I said, "I'm glad you decided to wait to sign the papers, Dan. It's better to take your time, so you know you're making the best decision for your life."

The words pulled out an emotional stopper.

"Best decision? I made my decision when we got married. She's the one who walked out. She's the liar! And I can't do anything about it."

"I know your wife's decision to move out with the kids isn't how you would choose to fix your relationship. Your wife pressed the ejector button and now you're the one in free fall."

"Yeah," Dan agreed.

"But what if you're targeting the messenger instead of the message?" I asked.

"What?" He lowered his gaze, eyes shifting down and to the side; he was thinking. Would he lash out again?

"You mean like in, 'Don't kill the messenger'?"

"That's exactly what I mean. Maybe your wife is the messenger telling you something's not working in your relationship."

To emphasize the point, Joe pulled out a prop we like to use for group.

"You see this little contraption?" Joe asked. "It's called a Chinese finger trap. Try it."

Joe handed him what looked like a collapsible straw made of woven paper.

"Now stick your index fingers in each end."

Dan complied, saying, "Okay, now what?"

"Now pull them out."

Dan pulled and the trap tightened.

"This is as far as I get without breaking it."

"Okay. So what happens when you try to pull your fingers out?" Joe asked.

"It gets tighter."

"Is it a pleasant feeling?"

"No. It's cutting off my circulation."

"Okay, now stop resisting."

"Stop pulling?" His skin was turning white just above the knuckle.

"Yes," Joe said. "Move into the tightness for a second."

Dan pushed his two fingers in and the trap loosened.

"I knew that would happen." Dan smiled, looking sheepishly at the other group members.

"Don't worry Dan," said Pam, the mother hen of our group. "They have us all do that one."

Dan smiled and knitted his brows, saying, "I don't get it. You're saying I'm pulling when I should be pushing?"

"It's not really pushing versus pulling. It has to do with resisting." Joe said while walking over to the whiteboard. "There's a great saying I like to use with this trap." He wrote the words in big block letters:

WHAT YOU RESIST PERSISTS

I turned to face Dan, searching his expression.

"You mean I should stop resisting the divorce?" Dan asked. "Just sign the papers?"

"Stopping the resistance doesn't mean you dash home and sign the papers," I said. "It means you stop the struggle with your feelings so you can get to where you want to go."

"How do I do that?" Dan asked, his eyes searching mine as if I was holding some mystical secret.

"By living your life. It's what this group is all about. It doesn't happen overnight, but you will have some 'aha' moments."

"So you're saying I have to come back?"

We all laughed at the joke like close friends at a dinner.

Dan held up the trap. "Can I keep this? I want to use it the next time my friend tries to swipe my cigarettes."

After the group session, Dan stayed behind to ask for individual help. Early on in treatment he discovered he'd fallen prey to some destructive myths about divorce that created a fog of war between him and Leigh. When Dan lost hope for saving the marriage, Leigh became the enemy. When he thought there was still a chance, she was his lifeline back to a loving family. Holding on to faulty relationship maps was like pretending the earth was flat;

not only was it wrong, his positioning system was steering him in the opposite direction of where he wanted to go. It made him reactionary instead of proactive. A victim battered by Leigh's unpredictable and sometimes, very predictable, actions.

Learning how to stop resisting starts with observation. Take a moment to consider what the struggle between you and your spouse looks like right now.

In our group sessions, we like to write down a list of things people commonly resist during divorce and separation, including physical, psychological, and social forms of resistance that go beyond specific interactions with a spouse, like:

- ☯ Binging on food or TV
- ☯ Abusing alcohol and drugs
- ☯ Smoking
- ☯ Isolating from friends and family

A Word About Exercises

You could leave your future to chance or take action. All the exercises in this book will help you look ahead and take a single step toward a greater truth. Don't push yourself too hard. At the same time, DO push yourself to work on the exercises that you naturally feel like skipping. Avoidance is one of the ways our mind protects us from the things that frighten or strike too close to home. Those are the exercises you will benefit from most because they tap into your blocked strength.

"Your vision will become clear only when you can look into your own heart. Who looks outside, dreams; who looks inside, awakes."—Carl Jung

Exercise: The Change We Resist, Persists

Here are some comments our group members have made about their own resistance. Check the ones that best describe your situation and add at least two of your own.

- ☐ "I resist taking time for friends. I feel so overwhelmed with work and parenting, I consider friends a luxury."
- ☐ "I resist asking my family for help. It makes me feel like I can't hack it. And what if they say, 'no'?"
- ☐ "I resist getting a babysitter. I feel angry. I have no money, and my husband should be doing it."
- ☐ "I resist doing things for myself. Like eating right and exercising."
- ☐ "I resist talking about my divorce."
- ☐ "I resist losing my wife. I keep telling myself there's got to be a way to save the marriage. I just have to try harder."
- ☐ "I resist letting my husband come into my house. He left me and the kids. He has no rights as far as I'm concerned."
- ☐ "I resist accepting what he's done to my kids. They don't deserve to grow up without a dad. He just slides in and out as he pleases and I'm the one that has to watch them suffer."
- ☐ "I resist sharing my real thoughts with my wife. She takes everything the wrong way, and it always leads to some bullsh-t argument."
- ☐ "I resist my feelings. They get so intense. I can't stand feeling like this. Drinking calms me down."
- ☐ "I resist letting her call the shots. I resist waiting. I need to know what's going to happen NOW, not two years from now."

Add yours below:

- ☯ I resist ____________________

- ☯ I resist ____________________

- ☯ I resist ____________________

Exercise: My Divorce is a Sign of...

Your unconscious is always in the background. Like a utility program on your laptop, it monitors your energy usage while juggling between active and sleeping programs. Like a program, your mind uses scripts to run your activities. You have a divorce script. It generates a code about divorce and what it means. Before you read on to discover some of the myths of divorce, take some time to tap into the scripts you have running in the background. This exercise allows unconscious thoughts to become conscious, the code to be decoded.

Let's explore some of your divorce scripts. Write down three things you think your divorce signals to the world and why you believe each to be true.

For Example: *My divorce is a sign of failure.*

- *I believe this because marriage is supposed to last forever and when it ends before forever, it means I've failed. Mission not accomplished.*

1. *My divorce is a sign of* ________________________________

   - *I believe this because :* ________________________

____

2. *My divorce is a sign of* ________________________________

   - *I believe this because :* ________________________

____

3. *My divorce is a sign of* ________________________________

   - *I believe this because :* ________________________

____

Give yourself time for this exercise. Writing about the beliefs that guide you exposes them to sunlight so you can start to see the cracks and faults in some of your assumptions.

Chapter Two Lessons:

- The divorce you resist, persists
- The stories we tell ourselves become our truth—even the fairytales
- A notice of divorce comes with a message, "There is something wrong with our relationship."

Chapter 3. Exposing the Seven Deadly Divorce Myths

"I was so panicked about losing my marriage, I couldn't see the gifts right in front of me." Hector G., hospital administrator

Let's take a look at some of the common myths that can fuel your suffering during a breakup. By drilling down to the core of these myths, you can go farther and faster in your acceptance of this new reality. These fake outs hover in the air like holograms in a movie theater, appearing to follow your movements. But try grabbing hold of one and you'll see it's like grasping at a shadow. Fortunately, you can unplug from each myth and just like a hologram, you can shut down its power to distract you on the way to committed action. The work you do to break through your assumptions about divorce can be the relationship gift that keeps on giving.

Myth #1: All my sacrifice is wasted.

Marriage is a practice in compromise and you've made your fair share of sacrifices for the good of the relationship. Some of the things you gave up might not even seem like a big deal. Like throwing away your favorite sweatpants because your husband thought they looked trashy or giving up some fun on the computer to spend more time together. Other sacrifices were probably more of a marathon than a sprint, like setting aside a career to take care of the children. You feel as if something that could have made a real difference in your life is lost. Maybe you put off that college degree you always wanted, believing if your spouse went first your turn would come later. You might be telling yourself it was all futile, that you've lost so much and you can never get it back.

Let’s agree that you sacrificed something really life-changing for your marriage. Does divorce mean your sacrifice is wasted like a bad stock purchase? Sacrifice is one of the highest expressions of love. It’s only when things fall apart that we realize how unpredictable all investments are, whether in marriage, parenting or the stock market.

“Sacrifice” is a word combination taken from two Latin words, “sacer” meaning “holy” and “ficium” meaning “to make.” Technically then, to sacrifice is to make holy or to do something which is holy. But there is also a modern definition for sacrifice which means “to permit injury or disadvantage to, for the sake of something else.”

So which is right? Did your sacrifice make your efforts holy or cause injury? Henry Ford once said, “Whether you think you can, or you think you can’t, you’re right.”

You can choose to believe that you are injured and at a disadvantage as a result of your sacrifices. Thinking of your time as wasted adds a layer of bitterness to your sacrifice and dishonors the value of your devotion to your marriage. Resentment transforms your holy act into a mishandled transaction, a poorly bartered deal. You can choose to believe that your gifts have sanctified your efforts. If your actions have strengthened your character or helped you see the value of your love, then you have honored your commitment, regardless of whether your marriage ends or flourishes.

“But, how can I walk away when I’ve lost everything?” It's a legitimate rebuttal, and in fact, the question drills down to the heart of this book. The truth is, you don’t have to walk away, and you don’t have to lose. Nor do you have to fix anything. For now, you are still on a journey, striving to get a better view of the terrain before making any long-term relationship decisions. Taking time to respect your sacrifices and to see the big picture doesn’t discount your heartbreak, but it does provide a new vantage point.

Case Study: Brenda's Sacrifice

Brenda came to divorce group with a history of sacrifices. She was eighteen when she was awarded a scholarship to study foreign languages. She dreamed of becoming a Foreign Service Officer. Growing up in an economically disadvantaged family, where no one had ever finished college, she was going to blaze her trail in a profession her parents had never heard of.

"Someday I'm going to be a U.S. Diplomat!" she announced to her father.

He had always encouraged her to set her sights high, and this was a rocket-sized liftoff. But Brenda's doubts grew heavy. She was afraid she'd dreamed too big. When her boyfriend, Jim, asked her to marry him, the decision was simple. She was in love and school could wait. Instead of pursuing the scholarship, she switched gears and accepted the position as Jim's wife. It was very exciting. Jim convinced her he could do anything. After his graduation from medical school, he joined the Air Force. Five years later, Brenda was staying home with three kids while Jim managed a hectic Emergency Department. She did her part. She cooked for the parties, hosted the dinners, and made friends with Squadron Commanders and their wives to improve her husband's chances for promotion. Brenda wasn't a very social person by nature, but she knew that networking was the secret to moving up in the ranks. She became good at making friends in high places, and it helped Jim get promoted. After 25 years in the military, Jim achieved the rank of Colonel. It meant great pay and a retirement that would easily pay all their bills. With her husband close to the end of a stellar career and the kids out of the house, Brenda was looking forward to their new life together. She started a Pinterest page storing images of all her travel dream destinations.

One night over dinner, Jim was unusually quiet. He'd been emotionally distant for months, but Brenda assumed it was because of the long hours he'd been working to train his replacement at the hospital. They were eating in silence when Jim got a text. Brenda poured herself a glass of iced tea while she waited, afraid it was work again. But when Jim looked up from his phone, he looked happy.

"I'm sorry. I've got to go."

"Work again?" Brenda asked, thinking how good it was going to feel to leave all that behind when they retired.

"No. It's not work." He fumbled with his words, "I didn't mean for it to happen, but I can't change it now. It's Cara. She needs me. I have to go."

In divorce group, Brenda explained that Cara, the "other woman" was a 32-year-old resident her husband had been mentoring for the past year.

"She's 20 years younger than me… 20! And he's taking advantage of his position, like some pig you'd see on TV! He told me that I don't stimulate him anymore. Hell, I barely have time to watch the news. Yeah, maybe I've gained some weight, and I don't wear Victoria's Secret, but that's the price we paid. Now, it's just me— paying."

Brenda felt devastated and betrayed. She'd kept her part of the bargain and worked through the hard times, the deployments, and the extra hours her husband spent on call. Now with the kids gone, she needed him more than ever, but he was nowhere to be found.

She had tears in her eyes as she told the group, "I was drinking coffee this morning, staring at the 'For Sale' sign on my front lawn and it suddenly hit me: I gave up all my dreams to make his come true."

It was time to check in with group. What did they think about Brenda's sacrifice?

"Her husband's an asshole," said Judy, a group member struggling with similar feelings of abandonment. "He doesn't deserve her."

Her comment opened up a flurry of responses.

"I say, she's got nothing to regret. Her kids have a great life, and it's 'cos of her sacrifice. She's leaving her mark for a long time." This was from a middle-aged man whose wife had already moved out of town with their children.

"I think she gets Karma points for her sacrifice," said a female college student who'd just joined the group. "Plus, she was just a kid when she got married. How can anybody blame her for a decision she made twenty years ago?"

"I think it depends on what Brenda takes out of it," said Dan, our Air Force engineer. "If she finds some meaning… something that helps her… then it's a good sacrifice. Otherwise, she'll have wasted all those years. Either way, I vote for fist-to-face therapy on her hubby."

Watching Brenda receive the comments from her peers, it was clear that she needed time to cope with the betrayal she was feeling. There was still time to grow through her pain.

Exercise: What Have You Given Up?

What did you sacrifice for your relationship and why? Did you give up a professional career? Did you put aside artistic pursuits or advanced education? Fill in the lines below with your own experience such as: "I wanted to write poetry, but there were bills to pay, so I got a practical job.

List three things you sacrificed for your marriage:

1. ______________________________

2. ______________________________

3. ______________________________

How do you feel about the sacrifices you made for the sake of your relationship?

____

____

____

____

Exercise: My Sacred Sacrifice

How have your sacrifices made you a better person? Do you value education more because you put it off? Are you secure in your capacity to love because you know you can give deeply to others? Has the pain you've experienced from your sacrifice given you a greater perspective on your life and your goals for the future?

____

____

____

____

____

The key to freedom is to realize that love is never wasted. The only thing wasted in life is the time you spend focusing on an unhappy situation that will never change to fit your needs, and not realizing the true investment of time and love are the lessons God wanted you to learn."

— Shannon L. Alder

MYTH #2. My spouse's life is going better than mine.

Do you feel like you're the one that's miserable while your spouse is happy and free? Now that you're separated, do you feel anger and resentment that they're getting what they want while you're being discarded? When someone does something wrong, they should be made to pay, right? It's like getting hit by a car and then having to pay for the offender's repairs. It's just wrong! What if I told you that you are more likely to grow from this breakup than your partner? You'd probably say that's hard to believe.

Lawrence Locker, a professor of Cognitive Psychology, and his colleagues at Georgia Southern University measured the recovery of divorce "initiators" and "non-initiators" (or more to the heart of it, the Leavers and the Left) and found that the myth that initiators recover more quickly was not supported by his research. Wouldn't that be ironic? You getting just as much, or more, out of the divorce than the person who thought they'd be better off without you?

In Zen Buddhism, there's a saying, "The Way is not difficult for those who have few preferences." There are studies that support the rationale that individuals who can shift with events outside of their control, live happier and longer lives. This is accomplished by letting go of expectations about how things "must and should be." When you feel outrage or bitterness over your breakup, it's because you had a roadmap of your life together. It had specific routes that lead to a destination: "We'll be together for life," or "Now that the kids are out of school, I can start my career." It's as if your spouse has hit the brakes and cancelled the trip without your permission. It doesn't feel good, but if you look past your injured feelings, you'll see that you have an infinite number of roads to choose from, based on *your* vision. Your spouse has committed to a specific path, drawn out of a desire to escape or perhaps a bit of fantasy. You, on the other hand, have been given complete freedom to explore.

Pearl: You're more likely to grow from the breakup than your spouse.

You will understand more about why you have a better chance of growing after you've read the upcoming section profiling "Leavers." For now, let's keep the focus on you. The Left start off in a basic struggle for survival. They've been blindsided by the Leaver and they're feeling helpless and unsteady. The Leaver has planned their escape for a while; they've had a chance to adapt, to plan, to map their path. In the beginning of the separation, the Left has a lot more work to do to regain their balance, but vulnerability and pain stimulate growth just like pruning the branches of a tree will multiply its blossoms.

Exercise: Stimulating Growth

1. Write down three positive changes you can make to support your life after separation.

Examples:

I am changing my priorities to make them more consistent with the life I want to lead.

I am paying attention to supportive relationships outside of my marriage.

a. ______________________________

b. ______________________________

c. ______________________________

2. List three positive things you can do now that you didn't do when you were living with your spouse.

Examples:

Inviting your friends over

Spending more time with the kids or pets

a. ______________________________

b. ______________________________

c. ______________________________

3. List three positive changes in the way you choose to look at your spouse. It's going to be hard work thinking up ways to extend compassion to your Leaver, but the work you do now to build compassion will help drain the acid that's burning a hole in your vision.

Examples:

____________ *(spouse's name) is pushing past other people's expectations about how he/she should live his/her life.*

____________ *(spouse's name) is telling me things they kept hidden before.*

____________ *(spouse's name) has her/his own path which is unfolding with each day. Neither of us know where it will lead.*

a. ______________________________

b. ______________________________

c. ______________________________

4. List three positive things your spouse does now that they didn't do when you were living together. (Skip this exercise if you have no contact with your spouse.)

Examples:

Buying his own groceries or cooking his own dinner

Spending more time with the kids

Taking time for her needs or wants.

a. ______________________________

b. ______________________________

c. ______________________________

MYTH #3: My spouse has stopped loving me.

So you've just gotten off the phone with your ex and you're still hurting from the things they said:

"I don't want to be with you."

"You need to sign the divorce papers now because nothing's going to change."

Does this kind of rejection prove they don't love you anymore?

Amicable divorces are very rare. I have treated many patients who were the Leavers, but mostly, it's the people who are Left that seek therapy. There's a reason for that, the majority of Leavers have had time to think about their decision. Many still love their spouse but are convinced their marriage or their life is intolerable as things stand.

Leavers see their marriage as the source of their unhappiness and decide there is only one solution: escape. But there's a catch. The Leaver is still emotionally connected to their spouse. In fact, the Leaver's anger, rejection, and overall disagreeableness are all signs of this attachment.

It may be hard to believe this, but your Leaver is probably more involved with you right now than they were in your day-to-day relationship. How could that be possible? Let's explore.

To understand what might be happening with the Leaver, consider this maxim by Nobel Peace Prize winner, Elie Wiesel:

"The opposite of love is not hate, it's indifference."

What does that mean? If love is truly kind and patient, and as warm and fuzzy as we are taught in I Corinthians, then isn't hate, with all its sharp daggers and rejection, the mirror opposite of love? Well, yes, but a mirror is still a reflection of the original image. For an emotion to be the true opposite of love, Elie Wiesel argued that the strength of feeling, the tie that binds, can't remain. Why? Because love and hate, are strong emotions that keep us hooked to the object of our love or hate. During the early stages of divorce, it is common for the Leaver to say hateful things on the way out the door. Straining for a quick escape, the Leaver bolts like a horse running from a burning barn: "We need to get this over with right away."

The words have an urgency that can sound almost hysterical. But ask yourself, Why the hurry? If your spouse is so removed from their loving feelings, wouldn't it be smarter to take some time to get things right? Wouldn't it make more sense to work out the best settlement? Or at least take it slow enough to reduce the impact on the kids or other loved ones? If logic, instead of emotion, were driving the process, the Leaver would manage the problem with a reasoned and reasonable plan. Pushing for a lightening-speed divorce, when there are so many critical decisions to be made (legal paperwork, distribution of property, preparing the family), is not evidence of rational behavior. Such hasty decisions are the smoke of hot emotions, not cool reason. Most of the time, the motivation is simple–a desire to escape. Escape what? Escape pain. Yes, there is pain, even for the spouse who is doing the leaving.

A patient of mine who was seeking a lightening-speed divorce once told me, "I need to get this tooth pulled quickly, or it's just going to keep hurting."

His words explained something about the Leaver's state of mind. Even though he had made the decision to leave his wife and had already moved out, he was still hurting. Why? Because he hadn't stopped loving her, despite his decision to end the marriage. Many Leavers try to run away as fast as possible because they're afraid of the intensity of their emotions—and yes, these emotions include love.

Some Leavers worry about losing their resolve, "What if I change my mind, lose my nerve? Then I'll be stuck."

When your spouse stuffed their clothing into a suitcase and moved out, they were fleeing. From your perspective, it might have looked like pure cold-hearted rejection, maybe even hatred, but at the core, the need to detach is your spouse's way of saying, "This hurts too much. I need to make it stop." As long as it hurts, it means your spouse is still connected, quite the opposite of the indifference that marks the absence of love.

How are you reacting? Are you feeling angry or enraged? Does that mean you have stopped loving your spouse? Of course not. Your anger, and perhaps hatred, is fueled by your own pain. How do you feel about a stranger? Does it break your heart when they say goodbye and walk away? No. Because you feel indifferent with a stranger. There is no love to connect you emotionally. The strong emotion we call hatred is just the opposite face of love on a coin called "attachment."

Ironically, some spouses believe they must go through the ritual of divorce to "reset" the marriage. They say hateful things, or whatever it takes to end their attachment, to cut the strings that tie the two hearts together. They may even start divorce paperwork on the hope that a new relationship will grow like a pine tree that sprouts from the seeds of an exploding pine cone after a forest fire. The idea is for love to grow freely, not out of obligation. Divorce is often a last ditch effort by a spouse who feels powerless to create change within the marriage. It's a powerful message about how love can survive even after a legal divorce. It is not an admirable way to bolster the marriage, but it helps to understand the motivation for those Leavers who seem to be saying, "I'm afraid of what will happen if our relationship doesn't change." Regardless of your Leaver's particular motivations for leaving, it helps to remind yourself that you are worthy of being loved.

Case Study: Celia's Last Laugh

Celia's husband, Jeff, was having an affair and decided to divorce. His girlfriend told him she couldn't be with him while he was still married, but Jeff kept putting off the leave date. One day, Celia came home unexpectedly. She had forgotten to pack her uniform for work in her mad dash to get out the door. She walked into the house and heard a woman laughing. She followed the sound and found her husband in bed with their next-door neighbor, a woman she considered a close friend. She felt shocked and horrified. In a particle of time, her world exploded. She ran past both of her betrayers to throw up in the bathroom. That one moment destroyed everything she thought she knew about her relationship. Even worse, Jeff didn't apologize or even try to explain. He simply said, "I can't do this anymore. I'm outta here."

In group, Celia sat crying with a growing pile of crumpled tissues on her lap.

"I can't believe it. He acted like I was the one hurting him!"

Jeff had pressed Celia for a quick divorce. He said he needed to be free. He didn't want to have to hide his relationship anymore. At first, Celia resisted, but in time, she stopped fighting the divorce. She turned to the people who cared about her for support. In the meantime, Jeff kept looking for Celia in his new lover. He'd argue with his girlfriend for being so jealous and possessive: "Celia never ragged on me like you do. We're not even married. I don't owe you anything." Jeff and his girlfriend eventually broke up, and he found himself alone in a studio apartment. Jeff and Celia had two dogs that they agreed he could take out on the weekends. Jeff noticed Celia was always dressed up and on the way out when he came over for "visitation" with their two Cocker Spaniels. She looked happy. He eventually started making excuses to come by the house more often: "Did I get a check mailed here?" He even offered to help with things around the house: "I noticed the light's out on the front porch. It'll just take me a minute to fix it."

Celia saw the change in his attitude and asked how his relationship was going. Jeff broke down and told her he had ended the affair. He said he realized how much he had lost by leaving Celia.

Did they eventually get back together? I can't say because Celia finished with group and moved on before making a decision. The point is that Jeff had never stopped loving Celia despite all his protests about wanting out of the marriage and finding a new love.

You can use Celia's story to pull back the branches obscuring the path ahead. Your Leaver may tell you the love is gone — burned to ashes and blown away. Seeing the scorched earth and smoke ahead, you may feel tempted to run for safety along one of those sure paths back at that fork in the road. At least you would know what to do, at least you would have a direction, either fighting for your marriage or choosing the escape route. But sure paths, like life, can be tricky things. Some are illusions that may lure you off a rewarding path. Follow your new map with a curious attitude. Keep your eyes open for landmarks that guide you in a positive direction, regardless of what your Leaver says.

Pearl: "The opposite of love is not hate, it's indifference."
- Elie Wiesel

Exercise: The Opposite of Love

This exercise will help you recognize whether there is still an attachment. Whether it feels like love or hate, write down the details of your spouse's behavior to help you identify their continuing level of attachment.

Examples:

My spouse seems uncomfortable when we're together.

He gets angry over the slightest thing.

She offers to help me.

He dashes out of the house soon after arriving.

She refuses to meet or talk.

____

____

____

____

____

Exercise: Is your Leaver acting with emotion or logic?

Emotion-driven behavior is easy to spot if you know the signs. Your spouse's actions are driven by feelings, especially when their actions seem unusually unpredictable and contradictory. One day they invite you to dinner or the park, and you have a reasonable conversation. The next day, they're spitting venom about what a terrible person you are. It's the love/hate coin flipping in a marital life or death struggle. You can refuse to get caught up in the chaos by standing back and observing without playing the game.

What is your spouse doing in pursuit of a speedy divorce? Label each of your answers as either logical (L) or emotional (E) actions.

Examples:

Selling the house under market value (E)

Conducting an inventory of possessions (L)

Stopping by the house unannounced (E)

Arranging for divorce mediation (L)

____

____

____

____

____

MYTH #4: Being apart means growing apart.

You and your spouse will be growing while you're apart, but that doesn't mean you're growing apart. Each of you still carries the other's voice around in your head, no matter how much distance stands between you. After being together as a couple, you have a good idea of how your spouse thinks. Consider this. How many times have you gone out with friends and known exactly what your spouse was going to say a few words into the start of a story? Could you finish their anecdotes? Your spouse has the same inner voice, hearing you in their head as they steer through their day. They might be fighting against it, but they can hear you even when you're not there. You don't have to be together to be connected.

I was out grocery shopping the other day while Joe was away on a business trip. We try to eat healthy, but Joe is more determined than I am. As I reached down for the bacon, I could hear him talking to me as soon as my fingers touched the slick, vacuum-sealed package: "Do you really want to load up on all that fat and cholesterol?" How is it that I carry my husband's voice around with me like Hal from *2001: A Space Odyssey*?

Over the years I've learned Joe's likes, his dislikes, and his thoughts in general. I don't physically need to be with him to have a good idea what he would say in almost any given situation. Even though you're not together, can you still hear your spouse in your head? Take time to think about that deep connection while you're apart. It will help you to stay grounded even when you're feeling abandoned.

Pearl: Growing while you are apart, doesn't mean you're growing apart.

Here's an argument for healthy time apart. Do you still get the same kick out of that great picture you hung on your bedroom wall when you first moved in? Do you look at it with the same fascination as when you first spied it in the store? Don't worry. It's not just you—we all do it. The psychological term for this phenomenon is "habituation." It's the same reason we suffer road hypnosis while driving home from work. We know where we're driving, we've done it a hundred times before. We slip into the driver's seat, put our foot on the gas and watch the sights blur by as we reflect on our day, steering on autopilot. Before you know it, you're home, but you've completely missed that majestic, hundred-year-old tree at the end of the block. It's always been there—you've just taken it for granted. The same thing can happen in a marriage. Whether you've been married for seven months, seven years, or seven decades, predictability can crush the passion that made things exciting at the beginning of your relationship. You wouldn't end your marriage as a means to renew it, but don't be so quick to see the time apart as the hangman's noose for your relationship. At the same time, don't be too hard on yourself for wanting to stay connected. It's human nature to hold on tight to the people we love. Keep in mind that during your time apart, you have a chance to see your spouse with new eyes—to consider the needs that weren't being met for both of you. Is that really such an awful thing?

Case Study: Dana's Internet Connection

When Dana and Conner divorced, he took a job as an English teacher in Japan. The job didn't pay much, but it did exactly what he wanted, it got him as far away from Dana as possible. Conner joked to his friends: "I wasn't looking for the opposite side of town, I was looking for the opposite side of the planet!"

Dana used the distance and time alone to start a Master's program in social work. Three months after their split, while she was doing her homework, Dana got an instant message on her computer from Conner.

Conner: Are you there?

Dana: Yes.

Conner: You're up late.

Dana: Not really—I do this all the time now that I'm back in school.

Dana kept working while Conner kept messaging.

In divorce group, she recounted her experience.

"At first I told myself, 'I'll be damned if I'm going to let him distract me from my schoolwork. He had his chance, and he blew it.'"

Try as she might, Dana couldn't help herself. She answered most of his questions and even asked a few of her own. The former husband and wife were now talking like pen pals. Typing on the keyboard seemed a lot safer than talking on the phone. Dana had learned that lesson after some heated exchanges before Conner had left to go overseas. Over time, the two shifted from messaging to talking. The first Skype call started innocently enough. They shared screens and passed each other funny memes and music files. Dana helped Conner with some of his lesson plans. Once his year-long contract in Japan was over, Conner decided to return to the States. The once-married couple started seeing each other again. It was like opening an old trunk in the attic; they had shared so many life experiences, it felt as if Conner had never left. They'd both hurt each other in their marriage, but they realized that they'd both helped each other more. The distance and time rewrote Conner's story about why he'd left, and Dana was glad for the chance to get her Master's degree.

Exercise: My Voice Will Go with You

Are you afraid of being forgotten during your time apart? As you go through your day, notice the times you hear your partner's voice. You might hear them reminding you to check the oil in the car, to "step away from the sausage," "change the cat litter," or "stop complaining."

Write down examples of the familiar voice in your head that keeps you connected even though you're apart. Now, remember, if it's happening to you, chances are, it's happening to them. And the more years you have together, the more often it's happening.

____

____

____

Exercise: Time Apart to Grow

Time on your own can be a valuable thing. Still not convinced? Look for the pattern. For example, do you argue when you are face-to-face or on the phone trying to work out a problem? Do you regret picking up the phone just to say "Hello" because it ends in a fight?

Write down the date and where you were the last time you and your spouse got into a disagreement. Make a sticky note for each time you get into an argument and place the note somewhere you can see it before calling or answering. Observing the direct relationship between your contacts and the disharmony that follows will help you realize it's time to let out the rope.

____

____

____

Think of the separation as a chance to see yourself as a whole person, to build up your strengths in a way that adds new life to the old picture hanging in your bedroom.

"We grow apart because we grow in different stages and not all of our stages align." – Dominic Riccitello

MYTH #5: My spouse has left me.

It might seem pretty clear that your partner is leaving you when they say, "I don't want to be with you anymore," or "I don't love you." It's normal to feel vulnerable, unlovable, and even helpless in the face of such unflinching rejection. Like Adam and Eve, it may feel like you've done something so unacceptable that your partner, like God, has cast you away from paradise as punishment. It hooks right into the fear that you are flawed. In response, you tell yourself to toe the line, to avoid making waves. If you just "act right" you'll get to stay in the garden. But let's push past the feelings of rejection to get at a kernel of truth. Your partner is not rejecting you. Your partner is rejecting the relationship. This is a crucial concept so stick with us here. It is the *relationship* that is unraveling.

Consider the following:

You're a whole person. Your partner is a whole person. You are both independent people who, at one time, decided to form a committed relationship. This relationship is separate from the two of you. By understanding and believing that the relationship is a separate entity, a whole in and of itself, you can begin to untangle the effects of your interactions. Accepting the difference between your partner leaving you and your partner leaving the relationship is essential if you are to regain your balance in the face of what looks like personal rejection.

PEARL: Your spouse is not leaving you. Your spouse is leaving the relationship.

We are so accustomed to thinking of ourselves as "one" with our lover that we can lose sight of the third factor—the relationship. But in fact, the relationship is the only thing that ties you together. The relationship combines your two individual actions (action/reaction) into an interaction. There can be no interaction, just as there can be no relationship without two people. More accurately, the problem exists not in you or your mate but rather, in your interactions.

If you're having difficulty with this concept, answer this question: Do you think, feel, and behave the same way with your spouse as you do with your boss, your mother, your mother-in-law, your best friend, your brother or sister? Most people don't.

Our relationships change according to the personalities, expectations, levels of intimacy, and the trust you bring into each interaction. That's why you might hold your tongue when your boss asks you to work late, but you have no trouble telling your best friend how much you hate working late. There are lots of things that determine how we feel and act in our relationships, but one thing is for sure: you need at least two people for an interaction. For this reason, you don't have to accept the myth that your spouse is leaving you, even if they literally say the words, "You're the reason I'm leaving."

Your spouse may believe that you're the reason for their unhappiness, but now you can listen with sharper ears, knowing that actions and reactions define your marriage. Take an extreme example from the play by Neil Simon, *The Odd Couple.* Felix is a neat freak, and Oscar is a slob. If Felix lived alone, he would happily keep things in perfect order, making sure he had a place for everything and everything in its place. Oscar, living alone, would merrily throw his sandwich wrapper on the floor and spill beer on the carpet on the way to watch the game in his bed littered with newspapers and old cigar butts. Put them in the same house together, and now you see the effect of their relationship. Felix is honking at Oscar, "Get your feet off the coffee table!" Oscar is shouting back at Felix, "Lighten up!"

The interaction is what creates the tension between the Odd Couple, and since neither of them is likely to change, the sparks keep flying and we, the audience, keep laughing. Felix may say, "It's your fault for being such a slob!" Oscar may say, "It's your fault for constantly nagging me." Each points the finger at the other, but we know that it's the relationship, that clash between opposites that is causing the conflict. The play is a comedy, but in real life, our conflicts can feel like tragedies.

There is such a thing as relationship synergy in which the whole is greater than the sum of its parts. One plus one can equal more than a happy couple. Felix plus Oscar equal more than two people living in the same space. If Felix moved in with another neat freak, the interactions would look very different. Recognizing the importance of the interaction effect in your relationship will help you look beyond personal criticism to build a strategy to stay centered while growing from your pain.

Case Study: Brian uses synergy to his advantage.

Whenever Jamie felt threatened during a disagreement with her husband, Brian, she would pack her things and threaten, "This time I'm leaving for good."

In the past, Brian would try to talk her out of it by saying, "Please, can't we just talk it out? I don't want you to go. I'll do whatever you want, just don't go."

Once, Brian even tried standing in Jamie's way to keep her from leaving. That was a mistake. Like a trapped animal, she lunged toward him with such force, he lost his balance and twisted his ankle.

Brian decided that the next time they had a disagreement, he would focus on the relationship. It didn't take long before he got a chance to practice. It happened on a Sunday morning just before church. Brian had invited his family for dinner. Jamie was nervous about impressing his mother who always seemed to find something wrong with their house.

As they dressed for church, Jamie asked Brian, "Did you remember to buy corn for the cookout?"

"I forgot," he answered.

"No way. I asked you for one little thing, and you couldn't be bothered. I've had it! You're so selfish." Jaime yells when she feels anxious. Within seconds she headed straight for her suitcase. "You can feed your parents on your own. I'm leaving."

Brian reminded himself that he did forget to buy the corn, but Jaime's angry flare-up was her own. Like an awkward dancer, he could lose time with the beat but Jaime, as his partner, could make up for it by keeping time with the music and letting him catch up. He used the dancing metaphor to focus on the interaction and to help him do something different this time. He stepped back long enough to show respect for Jamie's fears while releasing his own feelings of anger and rejection. By feeling more in control, the situation became less threatening to him, and he was able to show compassion for Jamie.

"I understand you're angry that I forgot the corn. I should've written it down before I went shopping, but it doesn't mean I don't love you." He moved away from her path out of the bedroom and offered, "If you need to leave, I won't stop you. But I'd like to work this out when you're ready."

Jamie watched Brian out of the corner of her eye, as he went on getting ready for Sunday service. He wasn't begging or forcing her to stay, but he had clearly expressed his wishes. The power struggle was over, the dance of anger and inadequacy halted. Changing his action created a different reaction in the relationship. Jamie put her overnight bag in the closet, got the car keys, and said, "Let's just go. I don't have money for a hotel."

Notice that Brian didn't say, "I'm sorry you're so upset with our relationship." He didn't need to convince Jamie that the relationship was the problem. He just had to remember that the conflict was between the two of them. As long as he trusted in himself as a worthy individual contributing love to their relationship, he could bounce back from the conflict in spite of his wife's accusations. By holding on to what was true for him (his love), he was able to avoid falling into Jamie's attack trap. Jamie never knew about the reframe going on in Brian's mind, but it made a big difference in the way she responded.

"The meeting of two personalities is like the contact of two chemical substances: if there is any reaction, both are transformed."
– C.G. Jung

The following exercise will help you see the difference between your spouse's actions and your reactions, the unique interplay that exists between the two of you. You both play an important role in your relationship. If you can step back and look at the interplay, you can identify the parts that are under your control and react in a non-threatening way that gets to the heart of the conflict. To do this, you must learn to respect the differences between your two points-of-view. Release the urge to fire back accusations in defense of your position. This isn't about you, it's about your *relationship*. Breaking it down according to your roles helps create perspective so that you don't assign all the responsibility (or blame) to one individual.

Exercise: Managing Your Reaction

Circle the best response to your spouse's statements:

1) Your spouse says, "You're always criticizing me."

    a) "You seem to be sensitive to rejection."

    b) "Are you kidding me? You're the one who's always criticizing *me*."

    c) "Well, I wouldn't be so critical if you weren't such a loser."

    d) "I don't mean to sound critical. What would be the best way for me to tell you when something is bothering me?"

2) Your spouse says, "You're the reason I can't be happy."

    a) "Who are you kidding? You wouldn't be happy if you won the lottery!"

    b) "What have you done to make yourself happy lately?"

    c) "I've been a terrible husband/wife. I should have done more to make you happy."

    d) "It's important to have joy in your life. What kinds of things make you feel happy?"

3) Your spouse says, "I don't find you attractive anymore."

   a) "Look in the mirror, buttercup. You're no movie star, either."

   b) "Have you seen the doctor? They say men/women your age often suffer from sexual dysfunction. Maybe you need a pill."

   c) "I've never been attractive. I don't know why you've stayed with me this long."

   d) "What gets you excited?"

By now, you've probably guessed that "d" is the correct answer to all the scenarios. They are not perfect answers but they work to diffuse the tension without assigning blame or invalidating the feelings. These exercises help you see that you can change the interaction. You may not feel comfortable saying the words in any of the suggested responses but that's not a problem. They're only meant to give you an idea of how to understand the interactions that form your relationship. You may be the target of your spouse's negative feelings right now, but it doesn't mean you're 100 percent responsible. It takes two people to create a relationship, two people to dissolve it, and two people to reconcile. You only have control over your part of the interaction, but your part can ultimately affect the greater relationship. Keep that straight in your head the next time you catch all the blame for the problems between you.

Exercise: Redirecting Common Reactions

Using the previous exercise, list some common statements your spouse makes that targets you as the culprit. What would you do differently if you refused to take it personally and reexamined the conflict as a relationship issue?

List new ways you could respond based on the knowledge that your spouse is commenting about the relationship, not you. Word your response in a way that would improve your interaction. The goal is to redirect your response by listening for the feelings behind the statement.

Spouse statement:

____

Relationship-focused response:

____

____

Spouse statement:

____

Relationship-focused response:

____

____

Spouse statement:

____

Relationship-focused response:

____

____

MYTH #6: I can't be happy without my spouse.

Happiness is like a butterfly landing on a flower—it lifts your spirits for a moment and then it's gone. When you attach your peace of mind to a single emotion, the clinging can squash the butterfly. Fear, abandonment, sadness, loneliness… all the negative emotions surrounding your marriage are the direct result of the attachment to your spouse. Notice the moments when you're having a particularly hard time; maybe crying, feeling outraged or isolated. Are those feelings a response to your thoughts about losing your spouse?

Your attachment creates heartstrings and we think of heartstrings as a synonym for deep connections. Sounds romantic, doesn't it? Now picture your heartstrings getting tight to the point of breaking every time your husband or wife walks away. After all, a string can only stretch so far. You mistakenly tell yourself that it's the leaving that's causing your pain, but it's your attachment. That string you've tied around your beloved is causing your agony.

Remember the old saying, "If you love something, set it free, if it comes back to you, it's yours. If it doesn't, it never was."? The problem with this little pearl of relationship wisdom is that no person is ever yours. Even if your lover does come back, they still do not belong to you—ever.

We don't just attach our happiness to people; we attach it to permanence, we attach it to stability. And yet, unplanned events happen in life and our expectations get turned upside down. Our thoughts, our bodies, our relationships--all are in flux. Emotions are too. Jon Kabat-Zinn coined the term "Full Catastrophe Living," adapted from a line in the movie, *Zorba the Greek*, to explain how life is full of changes. The good and the bad, mixing like sunshine and rain, create a full and unpredictable life. Sometimes you get that dream job and sometimes that dream job comes with a nightmare boss.

How many times were you convinced you knew how a situation was going to turn out only to be surprised by a sudden turn of events? You buy a dream house in an A+ neighborhood and discover your neighbor owns five St. Bernards that bark all night. Or, you walk into a restaurant that looks like a bomb shelter, after the bomb went off, and are served the best chili cheeseburger you've ever tasted. Life surprises all of us.

Full catastrophe living is a wife who excitedly puts on her helmet for a bike ride, even after watching her ex-husband drive off with his new girlfriend. Full catastrophe living is hearing that your mother is in the hospital and taking time to grab that snuggly robe she loves to wear so you can bring it with you to the hospital. Full catastrophe living is an enlightening experience because it embraces the fact that you have no idea what is going to happen in the future. None of us do. More importantly, it opens your eyes to what is. With eyes wide open, the world comes into focus, and you see ordinary things for the first time. You see people and events as they are right now, without bending them to your will.

When your marriage collapses, it's easy to create predictions about dying alone and unloved. But if you adopt full catastrophe living, the breakup takes on a different meaning. Your time apart means change. The outcome of that change is unpredictable, so you give up wasting energy on the things you can't control. You use the hole in your heart to make room for more love—love of family, love of friends, love of God, love of nature. Your heart was made to feel more than romantic love, and it is much bigger than encapsulated love for any one person.

Romantic love is like the illusion caused by an eclipse of the sun. The sun is 400 times wider than the moon but, when conditions are right, the sun's light can be completely blocked out by the moon. Does your attachment to your husband blind you to the love you already feel for your mother or father, your child, a good friend, your sister or brother? How does one person get so much power? The answer is, through attachment. Even an eclipse has a beginning, a middle and an end to the darkness. Attachment has no end until it's released.

Ironically, the sooner we surrender to the pain, the sooner we will know moments of happiness. The transformation begins the day we accept full catastrophe living, knowing that there can be no joy without sorrow, no relief without pain. Once we stop clinging to the delusion that we're supposed to seek out happiness and avoid distress, we free our mind.

People say that we only use 10 percent of our brain. Technically, that's not true, and there's plenty of research that proves it. But what if there's another way to understand that 90/10 percent argument? What if we only use 10 percent of our mind to see the world exactly as it is, without filters? That would mean that 90 percent of our mental activity is running on automatic, spurred by the programming that started when we were born. Scripts passed down to us by our mother, father, teachers, coaches, clergy and the rest of society have hijacked our ability to see things as they are. The 90 percent is so overpowering that we don't even think to question these "truths" handed down to us.

Pearl: Ninety percent of our mind is running on automatic.

Imagine a five-year-old girl is offered a lollipop. She sees the lolly and remembers how sweet the last one tasted. She makes a run for the man holding it out for her. Suddenly, Mom stands between child and man.

"Never take candy from strangers!" Mom admonishes.

The girl's mother just wants her child to avoid danger but the little girl learns that strangers with lollipops are dangerous. Mission accomplished. But is every stranger bearing candy a stand-in for Charles Manson?

Like a horse with blinders, the rules we learn about the world cover parts of our visual field. Pink Floyd called it "a brick in the wall." If, instead, we grew up in a society that encouraged us to look beyond automatic judgments of "good-bad," "scary-secure," "flower-weed," it would allow us to explore and discover truth instead of assuming it. When applied to divorce, it means that 90 percent of our mind is running on pre-written scripts about what the dissolution of a marriage means. But a sliver of our mind remains free to see our separation objectively, free of a distorted sense of permanence.

A small, distant light allows us to see the negative impact of attachment but the floodlight of assumptions can keep us blinded. Our false expectations can take on a life of their own so that fears become as real as any wild animal barreling down our path.

The Sad Zen Master

A Zen master was asked if he ever felt depressed.

"Yes," he answered.

His student was confused by the response and asked, "But you have reached enlightenment, how can you feel depressed?"

"Ripples in the water do not change the river," answered the master.

We accept the stories we've been told since childhood: "You can't be sad if you want to be happy," "Strangers are dangerous," and "Big boys/girls don't cry."

I sat down one day and considered all the unchallenged assumptions I carry around with me each day, like so many layers of fat they bog down my consciousness. Here's what I came up with in no particular order of relevance or even importance:

- ☯ My kids need me to be strong
- ☯ Work hard and study hard and you'll succeed
- ☯ More money means more security
- ☯ Love makes you strong
- ☯ Typing is better than hand-writing
- ☯ My house must be clean and organized
- ☯ Home-cooked meals show love
- ☯ Rich people have it easier
- ☯ Joe is responsible for putting the toilet seat down
- ☯ The best decisions take time and deliberation

These are just the ones that popped into my head. I walk around every day with thousands of these unchallenged beliefs, yet I know they would all be different if I'd grown up in another time, culture or social group. For instance, my millennial friends recently challenged me during a discussion about careers.

"You Boomers said that all we had to do was work hard and study, and we'd get jobs! Now we're broke with tons of student debt and no salary to pay for it."

I could argue that they're wrong and offer examples of people who worked hard and got jobs but that would deny their reality. It would be my 90 percent battling with their empty pockets. Neither of us would be paying attention to that 10 percent of our mind that can see the world and the job market is constantly changing, with no magic formula for success. Suspending the 90 percent part of my mind that needs to be right, would allow the 10 percent to listen and to see how technology has changed the job market, so that experience and productivity can be more relevant than formal education. To see the truth, I must be willing to start with the premise that I could be wrong. My 90/10 rule of mind activity reminds us why it feels so hard to break out of our normal mode, automatically believing every lure our mind flashes before us.

Khalil Gibran, the famous philosopher and poet, was one of those rare enlightened minds that saw truth where others never thought to look. In his book, *The Prophet*, Gibran rejected the belief that sadness is the enemy of happiness. His poem compares joy and sorrow using an image of the two pans on a weight scale. When one pan rises the other falls, they can never move independently. He rejects the social programming that demands that one emotion be better than the other, as if one leg or one ear could be more important than the other:

"Your joy is your sorrow unmasked.
And the selfsame well from which your laughter rises was oftentimes filled with your tears.
And how else can it be?
The deeper that sorrow carves into your being, the more joy you can contain.
Is not the cup that holds your wine the very cup that was burned in the potter's oven?
And is not the lute that soothes your spirit, the very wood that was hollowed with knives?
When you are joyous, look deep into your heart, and you shall find it is only that which has given you sorrow that is giving you joy.
When you are sorrowful look again in your heart, and you shall see that in truth you are weeping for that which has been your delight.
Some of you say, "Joy is greater than sorrow," and others say, "Nay, sorrow is the greater."
But I say unto you, they are inseparable.
Together they come, and when one sits alone with you at your board, remember that the other is asleep upon your bed.
Verily you are suspended like scales between your sorrow and your joy.
Only when you are empty are you at a standstill and balanced.

We attach ourselves to many delusions. We tell ourselves the sorrow we feel will stop us from feeling happy. We attach our heart to a person and believe our sorrow will persist as long as we're apart: "If only he'd come back, then I'd be happy." Our attachment to permanence is based on false assumptions, that change is the exception and constancy is the rule. Clinging to how things are "supposed to be" blinds us to truth, feeds our sadness, and starves our happiness.

Three Steps to the Spirit
"There are three phases of spiritual growth," said the Teacher.
The earthly, the holy and the divine."
The student grew excited to learn more. "What is the earthly phase?" he asked.
"That is when the person sees a mountain and knows it is a natural elevation of the earth's surface with an altitude greater than a hill." Answered the Teacher.
"And what happens during the holy phase?" asked the student.
"That is when the person looks at the mountain and sees a symbolic path through the clouds and into eternal life."
Excited to hear about the divine phase, the student pleaded, "What happens when we reach divinity, oh wise one?"
"Ah. That is when the person opens his eyes and sees a mountain."

Exercise: Seeing Things as They Are

This practice will help you get a little exercise while training you to observe without judgment.

Go outside and look around. See the clouds as clouds, not as a clown's head or an elephant. When you see a tree, stop and look at it, search for a scent, touch the rough bark, listen for birds. The idea is to see your world with all your senses. Try to catch any stray thoughts that take you away from seeing things as they are.

When you're done, go back inside and write down everything you noticed about any thoughts or feelings that distracted you. Did you see something that reminded you of your spouse? Were you feeling sad because of your attachment? "This was our tree," or "These cherry blossoms would smell so much sweeter if she were here to share it with me."

Attachment places a wedge between you and the truth. Practice reminding yourself that living things, like the tree and your spouse, do not belong to you. The cherry tree exists apart from you and apart from your marriage. The blossoms give off a sweet scent, a gift for you to inhale and enjoy in this moment.

Exercise: How Do Your Attachments Blind You to Beauty?

Write down some attachments that block you from seeing the beauty around you. Not sure of the attachment? Think of a painful emotion you're feeling and your response to that emotion. Here are some examples:

My attachment to my spouse is keeping me in bed and all I do is stare at the lint under my blanket.

My attachment to my spouse is distracting me from seeing the love my kids are showing me.

____

____

____

Exercise: Release the Heartstrings

List three fun things you would do to improve your life if you stopped telling yourself that your relationship has to be fixed first. Think about things that make you happy that you've put off because of your focus on your marriage.

____

____

____

MYTH #7. Accepting divorce means accepting failure.

Society tells us that marriage equals "happily ever after." The church reminds us that we took a vow that should never be broken. Parents want us to stay married because they divorced. Or maybe they stayed married so you should, too. Our culture celebrates anniversaries like birthdays, each new year a grander token of our wonderfully stable lives. In this way, divorce becomes shorthand for failure. We learn from media and society that marriage should last forever and that people who are healthy and flexible, those who work hard and have good judgment, don't get divorced. The assumption behind all of it is that staying together forever is the healthiest response for all couples no matter how much things change, and no matter how much unhappiness.

What if the failure isn't in our flexibility but in society's demand that we remain in the box it has constructed and unfolded for us, dropping our love in and taping it shut so that the light of impermanence can't get in? Divorce as failure ignores the pain we feel leaving the familiar: our spouse… the vision we had for our future.

When I went through my divorce, I was so embarrassed I kept it a secret for months. I told myself I had to fix it before anyone found out. Looking back now, I see that my fear of failure made the divorce inevitable. I bought into the "Divorce is for losers" social programming. A friend of mine talking about his second divorce said, "I'm a two-time loser." That wasn't going to be me; I was going to hold on to my marriage and beat the odds. I spent so much time trying to force that Weeble to lay on its side, fixed on my goal of not losing, that I never stopped to look at the problem. Like a doctor who prescribes a medicine before examining the patient, I was in for trouble: "Here, take this Ibuprofen for your headache. It didn't work? Oh! Why didn't you tell me you have a brain tumor?"

It never occurred to me that my need to avoid failure was only propelling me faster toward the end. Like the first day I went kayaking with Joe. As we paddled down a crystal clear creek in northern Florida, he whispered, "Stop paddling, there's an alligator on your right." I heard "alligator" and my paddle went wild before I looked to see where it was. In my hasty attempt to get away, I paddled right toward that alligator! Thank God he was just as afraid of me as I was of him. He darted into the water between Joe and me. But the experience came with a lesson: The things we tell ourselves we cannot, must not allow, can rise to the surface hungry and bearing sharp teeth.

How does a person let go of a fruitless struggle whether it's physical or marital? Let's start with the alligator. What if I felt the panic (can't stop that because it's built into my nervous system) but used those alarms to get a better fix on its location. Okay, now that I see him, I realize I've got ten feet between him and me. Or, if I look and see he's really close, maybe I'll have to use the paddle to defend myself. Either way, taking a moment to see what I'm dealing with and what I have control over, gives me the best chance of survival.

That's fine for the physical, but what about marital survival? The answer is the same, and it's the reason for this book. Taking the time to really see what you're facing gives you the best chance of survival, whether it's surviving alone or within your marriage. And notice I included surviving alone. Accepting the truth that you are whole all by yourself will keep you grounded in reality. It will help you see clearly. Giving in to your fear of failing or to the fear of losing your marriage will only blind you to the crisis and limit the actions that are still under your control.

Let's look at the divorce-as-failure myth from the opposite extreme, and you'll understand why it's so important to reject it outright. Imagine you saved your marriage and got kudos from everyone around you. Your mother says, "You have the best marriage, darling!" Your neighbor says, "I wish I could have your life. How do you do it?" What a great feeling! Now, imagine how long that great feeling will last when you have the next big argument with your spouse. The praise from mom and Mrs. Kravatz falls flat; the warm glow lasts only as long as the next fear of failure. Time is not your enemy. Divorce is not your enemy. Once you stop struggling you'll see your options expand like a Chinese finger trap.

Case Study: Neil Accepting Change

Neil worked long hours and traveled for his job. One day, he came home from work to a huge shock. His wife, Cindy, had moved out and left him with their five children. She'd found a job as a teacher and a private home with an older couple where she could pay for room and board.

Neil asked, "Why didn't you tell me you were leaving? How am I supposed to take care of the kids by myself?"

Cindy said, "It wouldn't have mattered. You don't listen anyway." She told him to let the older teens take care of the younger ones. That's what she always did with him gone so often. She had discovered a new life. All she could talk about was how kind everyone was being to her. The husband and wife she rented from valued and respected her. She told Neil he was irritating. She didn't want anything more to do with him and the life he'd "forced" her to live. Neil was shocked and didn't know how to respond. He decided to take charge and win her back. He dropped off a bouquet of flowers at her new place with a simple note saying, "These flowers pale by your beauty."

His wife tossed the flowers in the garbage and called him in a rage.

"You're stalking me! I never said you could come here. This is my home!"

She threatened to call the police the next time he showed up uninvited. Neil couldn't believe what he was hearing. He shared, "I don't know who that woman is, but that's not my wife!"

He felt hurt and angry and had no idea what to do about it. He learned about our divorce myths and used them to keep himself steady during the months when he and Cindy lived apart. He decided it was best to give his wife time. He used that time to develop a plan with the older kids for getting through the crisis. He also asked his employer if he could work at home temporarily. To his surprise, he was allowed to work from his house for two days a week. Neil accepted invitations from his friends to go out on the weekends with the younger kids in tow. The teens were more inclined to go out with their own friends on the weekends. He also took a photography class three nights a week and became fascinated with taking pictures. A colleague saw his work and asked him to shoot his daughter's wedding. Neil was still grieving, but he worked hard to give Cindy the time and space she needed.

Cindy dropped by the house one day to deliver some paperwork. She commented on how neat and tidy the kitchen looked. He showed her the schedule of chores he had developed on a whiteboard with all the children's names on it and his own at the top. He caught her scanning the room.

"You're dressing better," Cindy told Neil.

Neil replied, "Yeah, I got some great stuff at Goodwill. Major brands."

"You always complained about me getting used clothing for the kids," she said.

"I did? Well, you were right—it's a great way to save money."

Neil was changing. He was focusing more on the kids now, and they appeared to be getting along fine without her.

Even though Neil and Cindy were still in the midst of a divorce, he'd decided he would create pockets of happiness on his own. He stopped focusing on getting Cindy back and made sure to listen without distorting her words with his fears. He stopped visiting unannounced. Most of all, he stopped resisting what had already happened. Instead, Neil shifted his focus to the things he still had control over and accepted the things he couldn't. Detaching from the things he could not control allowed him to adjust… and it showed.

Exercise: Creating a Truce with Failure

We are programmed to fear failure from the time we can understand language. "You have to learn your ABC's then you will be able to read and get good grades in school. Good grades will help you go to a good high school, maybe college." And so we learn to keep climbing the ladder of success, always avoiding failure. Failing is bad. By the time we become adults, the thoughts are automatic: there is no room for failure.

What if we reset the program? What if we blew away the stink of "bad" from failure and looked for the moral of the story. Then we would see that failure isn't the enemy.

Write down what divorce is teaching you:

Divorce is letting me know something isn't working

Divorce is opening the door to greater truths in my life

____

____

____

In the last myth, you practiced going out and seeing things as they are, without the color of your judgments. For this next exercise, you'll add a layer to the practice by seeing the person you married without attaching your needs to their words.

Think of the last exchange you had with your husband or wife. Pretend you're a doctor and your job is to listen to their complaints without judging them or being attached to a specific treatment.

Example: Your spouse says, "This isn't the life I want to live. I can't be with you anymore."

What can you see if you remove your attachment to an outcome?

Answer: "I see a person who looks frustrated with their life right now. A person who believes they have found a solution."

The more you can act as an observer without attaching your needs to your spouse, the more you will see and learn.

Exercise: Seeing is Not Judging

This is one of the hardest exercises, and many people want to put it aside because the attachment is still too strong. Have patience and stick with it for as long as you are able. Write down one of the reasons that your spouse says that they are leaving and then write down the emotions that you think your spouse is feeling:

____

____

____

Now that you've delved into the deeper longing, disappointment, or fear carried by your spouse, does it make sense to cover that window with the black paint of failure? It might be easier to block out the rejection but at the loss of a more profound understanding.

In this chapter, we've debunked some common myths that can cause suffering. Letting go of these distortions will help you to be more objective about the events that are dragging you down. Getting in touch with the truth will offer new directions. In the next chapter, you will learn some concepts and techniques to help you accept your partner's decisions while also respecting your own needs.

Chapter Three Lessons:

- ☯ You don't have to walk away or lose or fix anything. For now, stay open and observe.
- ☯ The person leaving the marriage has had time to decide, give yourself time to catch up.
- ☯ Pain stimulates growth the way pruning a tree multiplies its blossoms.
- ☯ Hate is not the opposite of love.
- ☯ Your spouse isn't leaving you, they're leaving the relationship.
- ☯ Attachment places a wedge between you and the truth.
- ☯ Divorce is not your enemy.

Chapter 4. Swimming To Calmer Waters

He just doesn't get it. I need him to leave me alone.
—Gabriella F., artist

When someone you love walks away, it hurts. You want answers. How could the person you trusted to stay for life be leaving— for life? It's tempting to feel outraged but that painful churning that's threatening to destroy your sanity is based on an illusion, the illusion that your spouse is yours forever with the power to snatch away your wellbeing without your consent.

How often do you tell yourself that you're a complete person and your spouse is a complete person without you? Rebuilding and respecting the boundaries that were set aside to accommodate your union during marriage will take effort. You're used to cooperation, a shared vision for the future, a reliable ride to the airport. Seeing a wall where there was once an open field can be jarring for anyone so if you find yourself looking for a sledgehammer instead of a ladder to get you past that wall, be patient.

~

Imagine you're at the beach, swimming in the ocean. It's a beautiful day; the sun is shining, seagulls are soaring overhead, and you're floating in gentle waves. You look over and see your spouse closer to shore. The crashing waves of the surf are pummeling them. Every time they try to stand up, another wave knocks them down and sucks them under the water. You swim over with the intention of pulling them out into the deeper water where the waves are smoother. As soon as they see you approach, they start thrashing. They look scared and motion you to go away. They are shouting now.

"What are you doing? I'm trying to swim to shore. Get away from me!"

You say, "I'm trying to save you."

As you swim closer, they thrash wildly, turning away from you and swimming toward the shore again. Along the way, they get taken down by another wave. You swim faster now. You know that if you can just get your arms around them, They'll realize that you can reach them ahead of any lifeguard. Everything will be fine if they will just stop resisting. You get close enough to wrap an arm around their waist and start swimming for the safety of the calm water.

"Stop it! Get off me!" they shout.

Your spouse is stuck in a struggle. They want out but the waves are too strong, and now you're adding to their dilemma. They can only see the shore as safety, heading for deeper water is not an option. What should you do?

Plan A. You could swim to shore, saying, "Go ahead and drown for all I care. I tried to save you, but you won't let me."

Plan B. You could keep swimming toward them insisting, "I know what you need more than you do."

Plan C. You could swim farther out into the water where the waves are smoother while they continue to struggle toward shore.

Does Plan C sound ridiculous? Maybe. But let's take a closer look. Your spouse is not enjoying their time in the water, a symbol of your relationship. They want out. The more you try to help, the more panicked they feel, and the more they resist. Pulling back and allowing yourself to enjoy the day in the calmer waters removes the conflict. Releasing your hold and allowing them to find their own way is much more constructive. It stops the cycle of control and the frustration it creates. They have the right to try and reach for the shore alone. Once there, they can sit on the sandy beach, catch their breath, and feel safe again. They are in control of their life. Eventually, they might look out over the waves and see you enjoying the day. The respect you show for your spouse's right to make decisions, and your own right to live free, can create a shift in the way you interact and appreciate one another.

Case Study: Dan and His Rescue Attempts

Dan was passing a pet store and noticed a litter of adorable tabby kittens. He'd always wanted a cat, but his wife didn't like them, so he'd given up asking. She'd say, "They're always jumping up on the counters with their dirty cat-litter paws." That day, snagged in the lure of those furry kitties, Dan indulged. He walked into the pet store and began stroking a little tuxedo kitten with a white breast and big blue eyes.

In divorce group, he shared his experience.

"It felt so good to play with that little fur ball. She was smaller than the others, and she liked me straight off the bat."

Dan described how wonderful it felt to stroke the kitten's soft fur. When she nuzzled under his chin, he was ready to peel all the bills from his wallet.

"I'd already called the sales guy over when I realized, I can't do that! It would be like slamming the door on my marriage."

Dan felt confused. He wanted the kitten for company, something to love and love him back. Touching her soft belly and feeling her lick his hand fed a skin hunger he didn't know he had. But there was no getting around it. A kitten would never fly with Leigh.

“So I called Leigh one more time to tell her what a big mistake she was making.”

Dan had phoned many times before, but he told himself that this time would be different. Leigh needed to understand just how much her desertion was affecting his life and their family’s life. He couldn’t believe she could be so selfish. He needed to convince her to come back to her senses and stop being so hurtful to everyone.

Imagine Dan in that ocean with his wife. He tells himself he’ll swim away next time, but for now, he’s got to give it just one more try. Dan feels frustrated. He’s tired of swimming through the same rough waves, but he just can’t break away.

Dan called Leigh and the response was predictable: “I told you to stop calling me,” she said. “We’ve already been through this. You’re just making it worse.”

Why does Leigh keep reacting the same way? Because, she has convinced herself that her life would be better without Dan. Every time he tries to tell her it could work, they are back in that surf with Leigh gasping for air. In her mind, Dan is offering an anchor, not a lifesaver. Just listen to some of the comments of other fleeing spouses and you’ll understand why rescue doesn't work:

“Susan just doesn’t get that I need space. She’s constantly checking on me.”—Sam, a mathematics teacher

“Carl acts like he cares now, but where was he when I needed him?”—Sarah, a physical trainer

“Roberta can’t accept that I’m in love with a woman who makes me feel happy. She keeps trying to make my life hell.” —Mike, an electrician

Your spouse wants to get away from the crashing waves—to stand on dry land, feel the sand between their toes, and breathe on their own. Without a struggle, the threats seem tamer. They can look out at the water and wonder, “Did I overreact?” By taking a break from rescue, you’ve presented your spouse with an alternative. It’s not that they can’t swim—it’s the constant pounding from the waves they want to stop. Without you to struggle against, the despair is all their own, and the bullseye on your chest is washed away.

Exercise: Water Challenge

Here are some examples to test your understanding of how to detach from the impulse to save your relationship. Place the letter "A" next to the statements that show your attempt to hold on to your attachment to your spouse. Place the letter "D" next to the statements that show you are able to detach, allowing you both to be free to make decisions.

1. Your spouse says, "I need to get away. I need some time to think." You reply:

    a. __ "Why don't I book us a night for two at a great hotel? It'll be a second honeymoon."

    b. __ "I understand. I'm going to sign up for a wine-tasting class at the college."

    c. __ "Why don't you let me take you out to dinner? I know you've been stressed lately."

    d. __ "It sounds like you need some downtime. Why don't you go do that favorite thing of yours? Don't worry about stuff around here. I've got it covered."

    e. __ "Take the time you need. I don't want to pressure you. I can always find stuff to do on my own."

2. Your spouse says, "The only thing that will fix this is a divorce." You say:

    a. __ "Divorce! No way. I'm not giving you a divorce no matter what happens."

    b. __ "A divorce is a serious step. I married you for life, but I don't want you to feel forced to be with me."

    c. __ "If you divorce me, I'll take you for every penny you've got."

    d. __ "I want to be with you, and I'll be sad if you leave, but I know it's just as important for you to want to be with me too."

    e. __ "I gave you the best years of my life, and this is how you repay me?"

3. Your spouse says, "I love you, but I'm not in love with you anymore." You say:

    a. __ "What can I do to make you love me again?"

    b. __ "I believe love is more than a feeling, it's a decision. But that's me—I can't tell you what to think."

    c. __ "But we just made love yesterday. You must have felt something."

    d. __ "Take your time to explore what love means to you. I don't want to force you to feel something you don't want to."

    e. __ "We just need some time away together, without the kids. Let's go tonight."

4. Your spouse says, "I'm in love with someone else." You say:

    a. __ "How pathetic!"

    b. __ "You must know you're in lust, not love."

    c. ___ "I'm hurt and we need to separate, but I'm not ready to make a rash decision about our marriage."

    d. __ "You can't give up on our life… our family!"

    e. __ "This is hard for me, but I won't be with you while you're with someone else."

Answers:

1. a = A, b = D, c = A, d = D, e = D
2. a = A, b = D, c = A, d = D, e = A
3. a = A, b = D, c = A, d = D, e = A
4. a = A, b = A, c = D, d = A, e = D

Exercise: When Rescue is a Rest Cue

Does your spouse seem more nervous or angry when you try to get close? Give examples:

____

____

____

Do you notice ways you are pushing to get your spouse to change their mind, to come back home? Give examples:

____

____

____

Make a commitment to give your spouse time to find his or her way out of the choppy waters.

My Commitment

I, _______________(your name) will make my most committed effort to allow __________(spouse's name) the time and space to find his/her way out of this crisis.
I will imagine myself swimming out to calmer waters as a way to interrupt my natural desire to rescue __________(spouse's name).
I commit to my growth as a means of improving my ability to have a good relationship in the future, with or without __________(spouse's name).
I will remind myself every day that I can't change __________(spouse's name), but I can change my focus and my reactions.
I will listen to __________(spouse's name) without judgment in order to understand his/her concerns.
I will focus on my growth as an individual.
By taking care of myself, I will be able to respond to __________(spouse's name) in more positive ways.
By responding with compassion to __________(spouse's name), I am increasing our chances of having a good relationship no matter what happens to the marriage.
By improving my ability to have a good relationship with others, I will feel happier.
I commit to finding happiness again in my life, with or without ________________ (spouse's name), in my own version of "full catastrophe living."

Signed,

It may seem like too big an effort to make and keep this commitment right now, but by the time you finish this book, you will have plenty of tools to help you. For now, it's important to make the commitment a priority by setting a goal to release your rescue efforts. Setting a goal is like activating a GPS for life. You have to identify an address in order to arrive at your destination. You may not know how to get there on your own, but you know that plugging in the address gives you a better chance of getting there. Let this book and your commitment to the miracle of your life act as your GPS. Don't forget, from time to time you will stumble and fail in your resolve. That's normal. But when you get sucked in by unrelenting habits, remember two things: don't beat yourself up for it, and get right back to the task of swimming in the right direction! Otherwise, you'll be like the lamb in Aesop's fable, trying to convince an unyielding wolf to change his mind.

The Wolf and the Lamb

A wolf saw a lamb that had strayed from the flock. He decided he wanted to make a meal of this lamb but wanted to justify his right to eat it.
He said, "Lamb, last year you insulted me."
But the lamb replied, "How could I? I was not yet born last year."
Then the wolf said, "You feed in my pasture."
But the lamb replied, "No, good sir, I have not yet tasted grass."
Again said the wolf, "You drink of my well."
Again came the reply, "No, I have never drunk water, for my mother's milk is both food and drink to me."
After hearing this, the wolf seized the lamb and ate it up, saying, "Well! I won't remain without supper, even though you refute every one of my concerns."

The moral of the story: Just like the lamb, it doesn't matter what you say once your spouse has made the decision to leave. Your best bet for survival is to disengage from debate.

Chapter Four Lessons:

- ☯ The belief that a person belongs to you is a delusion.
- ☯ Without your marriage rescue efforts to struggle against, your spouse's despair is all their own.

Chapter 5. The Autopsy Room

At first I didn't want to admit it, but marrying Reed made me feel important. —*Samara M., waitress*

The marital autopsy is a tool I developed to identify the behavioral causes of matrimonial death. The idea came to me from my work as a military psychologist, which required me to conduct psychological autopsies. Working with the Office of Special Investigations, my job was to review all the records pertaining to a service member's life when their death looked like suicide. I would research the person's history, read the suicide note (if there was one) and use every bit of data and communication to understand why that individual killed themselves. Faced with my divorce, the loss felt so much like a death that it seemed only natural to conduct the same kind of exhaustive review of the factors leading up to the end of my marriage. I call it a marital autopsy because it captures the finality I want us to establish before we start this investigation.

The word autopsy comes from the Greek word, autopsia which means "to see with one's own eyes." The marital autopsy you're about to perform will allow you to examine the causes of marital death and explore the extent of the dis-ease within your relationship. It will identify conflicts you have not recognized about your marriage. You will need to be brutally honest, even if it hurts, especially when answering questions like:

Do either of you have a history of infidelity?

Did either of you act abusively?

Diving into such a personal examination can be daunting, but there is nothing like seeing the truth for yourself. This is your work and no one else needs to know where it leads you. Slicing through the emotional layers will expose some potential truths about your relationship. Realities like:

- ☯ The relationship was already terminal; your spouse just had the guts to pull the plug first
- ☯ Both of you share responsibility for the death of the relationship
- ☯ You have power you don't yet recognize

Exercise: Reacting to the Idea of a Marital Autopsy

1. What is your reaction to thinking of your marriage as dead? Be honest about any anger or hard feelings that surface.

____

____

____

Case Study: Office Olivia

Olivia is a 33-year-old police officer in the Air Force, an SP for short. Although she was used to people respecting her orders on base, at home her husband, Nestor, refused to stay and work on their marriage. Olivia was facing a divorce that showed no respect for her authority. She tried to change Nestor's mind by using seduction, apologies, and when those didn't work, threats. She tried bribing him by signing over one of their savings accounts because he was short on cash one month. It was proof of her love. He withdrew the money the same day and used it for a 12-month lease on an apartment. When she heard the news, there was no more denying that her marriage was over; it was time to get on with her life. Her resolve lasted about a day before she noticed a twisting pain in her stomach. She knew this pain: "He's never coming back." Her next thought shoved the first one out of the way: "He doesn't love me anymore." Her chest tightened with each alarming blast from her brain ... then it got hard to breathe. Locked in a cycle of abandonment and rejection, she ended the night feeling completely out of control, telling herself she couldn't take it anymore. It was so unfair for him to leave without trying to fix things. There had to be some way to convince him he was wrong, some way to get him back, some way to stop the panic rising inside her like a whale breaching against her lungs. Getting him back was an act of self-preservation; there was no choice; she had to breathe to survive.

Is it wrong for Olivia to keep fighting for her relationship?

You learned in the last chapter that attempts to rescue your partner from the pounding surf only makes things worse, but the urge to recover your loss is strong. You want to stop feeling bad, and your heart tells you that getting back together will take the awful feelings away. But what if your heart is too focused on feelings? Like a driver who inflates a flat tire without realizing he's got a nail stuck in it, your emotions are trying to breathe life into a flat relationship without fully identifying the source of the problem.

Even with all her training as a police officer, Olivia's fears were so powerful, they took control. Panic guided her actions. Her husband's depletion of their entire bank account validated her feelings of betrayal and left her with less money to take care of her needs. Redirecting her efforts on accepting the loss, instead of directing her efforts toward recovering her relationship, would have given Olivia a chance to take control at a time when she was feeling the most hopeless.

Picture your marriage as a dead body lying on a stainless steel table in the hospital morgue. The last time you saw it was in the ICU, but now it's here, and there's nothing you can do to bring it back to life. All your CPR efforts have failed to establish a heartbeat. The doctor has called the time of death, and now it's up to you to perform the autopsy. You feel sick at the sight of your lifeless relationship, but there's also a peaceful stillness.

My own marital autopsy felt like I was pulling a wound packing off my heart. The relationship may have been dead, but my feelings were still pulsating wildly. Searching through my nightstand one night, I found letters from my husband explaining why he was so angry. I put those aside and started reading my notes to him along with my diary entries. I reconstructed conversations and events between the two of us and our families. I replayed mental images of the times he drew close, and the times he stormed away, writing down the facts as if I were John Gottman, the psychologist who famously brought couples into the laboratory for observation. By inspecting each vessel of the circulatory system that connected the two of us, I was able to identify conflicts I hadn't noticed before. The examination was like pulling out a magnifying glass and seeing the shrapnel that took out our marriage.

I learned so much from this form of dissection that I started using the marital autopsy as a treatment strategy with my divorcing patients. Later, I went on to develop a paper and pencil instrument assigning scores to the most common types of marital conflicts. Sometimes my patients made seismic discoveries, other times the autopsy just confirmed what they already knew but weren't ready to accept. Whether the insights were large or small, the deep analytical work of examining the marriage always moved the process of understanding forward.

Does the prospect of staring into the bare cavity of your relationship scare you? It's natural. You'll be taking a hard look at both your actions and inactions over the life of your time together. The unvarnished truth is bound to make you uncomfortable. You might even think it's morbid to talk about your marriage as dead. After all, your spouse is still alive. So, why say it's completely over?

Recall the myth that explained that your spouse is not leaving you but is leaving the relationship. Your old relationship is dead, it cannot thrive without two committed people. If you skip past this autopsy, you will be making three mistakes:

1. Acting as if your spouse belongs to you.

2. Attempting to rescue your spouse.

3. Missing important clues to why your relationship ended.

The sooner you face your new reality, the greater your chances of finding long-term happiness, with or without your partner.

As a partner in a marriage, you've had certain expectations. Those expectations can act like twenty-pound weights around your ankles, slowing you down, making the tiniest steps feel like a marathon. You can't afford the dead weight of old expectations anymore. Your marriage, as you've known it, has breathed its last breath. Holding on to the dead body keeps you in stagnation. If you are Christian, think of how Jesus died before he could be reborn. Almost all the world's religions have some version of an afterlife, whether in the form of heaven, reincarnation, rebirth, or a journey toward a new existence. All these faiths accept the reality of death as a means to a new, more radiant life. Let that hope strengthen you as you prepare for the examination ahead.

Spouse as Possession

We all have a tendency to see our spouse as belonging to us: "This is my husband/my wife." We announce it with pride at parties and with new friends. But the subtle message is also clear: "Mine… mine… mine. Hands off!"

We make statements such as:

"You belong to me."

"Be mine forever."

"I want you all to myself."

"You're all mine."

"You complete me."

Wedding vows include phrases like:

"To have and to hold from this day forward."

"And forsaking all others keep thee only to her/him, so long as you both shall live?"

How often have you thought of your spouse as someone no one else has a right to take from you? Take a moment. Does that really sound right when describing a grown adult?

"You belong to me" sounds perfect for Valentine's Day cards and romance novels, but it's based on a false assumption: that one person can be possessed by another. If the scene changed from a romance novel to Uncle Tom's Cabin, those same words would transform from lovely to ominous and there's a reason for that. No human being can ever belong to another.

All persons, including those who are married, must willingly submit to their bond, even when that bond is matrimony. There is a difference between bond and bondage; it's the freedom to go.

In slang, "the old ball and chain" is sometimes used by men to refer to a wife's capacity to limit his freedom. The ball and chain is literally a leg shackle attached to a heavy metal ball used to prevent prisoners from escaping. The reference is supposed to be funny, but like all jokes, it contains a kernel of truth: that a wife can shackle her husband by limiting his freedom. Women have a history of being shackled too. Just a few generations ago, wives were considered the chattel (property) of their husbands— same as cows, horses, and land. The legal designation of wives as chattel, along with the popularity of chastity belts, may be the starkest expression of our human tendency to possess our lovers. And yet, the desire to possess is at the root of human suffering.

> *There is a difference between bond and bondage; it's the freedom to go.*

Case Study: Julie's First Son

Julie's husband, Ray, had leased a studio apartment and packed his bags before he told her he was leaving.

"What? You're leaving… just like that?" Julie demanded.

She never saw the divorce coming. They'd been arguing more than usual, but Julie was secretly happy to see Ray acting more like an adult. He was standing up for himself lately, and she was feeling a stronger attraction. When they first got married, she'd felt more like a mother than a wife.

In the morning, as he got ready for work, she'd complain, "Why don't you dress better?"

She reminded Ray when to get a haircut and made sure he got out of bed on time for the commuter train. How would they save enough money for kids if he didn't get serious about his career?

Lately, he'd been doing more on his own, working late and staying in the city overnight instead of making the long commute back home.

In therapy, Julie said, "I thought we were moving in a positive direction. More hours at work meant more chances for promotion and more pay." She wiped at the flood of tears when the words spilled out, "But instead of thanking me, he turned into a different person."

In her mind, Ray had gone temporarily insane. She would not accept the idea that their life together was over. One day, she pulled into his apartment complex "just to talk." As she sat in her Toyota scanning for his car, she saw him pull into a parking spot and open the door for a woman in the passenger seat. Next, he went to the trunk and pulled out a grocery bag. She could feel her blood boiling as the woman took his hand on the way up the stairs.

"How could she do that? She must know he's married. What kind of skank would take a woman's husband like that? She has no right. He's my husband!"

The more she thought about it, the angrier she got. She thought about keying his car but thought better of it and drove away in tears.

Julie saw her husband as an extension of herself. His success was her success. Her goals were his goals. There was only one problem: Ray didn't care about money. At first, he pushed himself harder at work to please Julie, but over time, he became resentful. He was living her life, not his.

"You've turned me into a human pretzel, and I'm sick of it." he complained before walking out the door.

He hated getting up for work in the morning because he hated his job. When Julie nagged him for not getting up on his own, it made him feel like a man-child.

Do you think Julie would have treated Ray this way if she didn't consider him a possession, or more kindly, an extension of herself? Marriage as looking glass confines us to a small space with little option to move about freely.

Do you think Ray felt free within his marriage to pursue his values?

You might say, "Bull! Marriage is a commitment. A vow is a promise, and that means the free part is over. Ray should stay and work it out no matter what."

If you believe this about your marriage, answer this question: How is that line of thinking working for you? Is it creating an open path for a new relationship with your spouse? Is your partner responding positively to your vision of how marriage is supposed to work?

Here's an alternative question: What would happen if you shifted your line of thinking away from your spouse and toward the relationship itself? Maybe you were doing things to keep the marriage alive but expectations for a specific outcome caused them to backfire, like Olivia signing over the bank account with the goal of keeping Nestor at home. Maybe you trusted so much in the sanctity of your vows or the loyalty of your partner that you didn't see the winds shifting and the fidelity fading.

To start your autopsy, you'll have to check your feelings of possession at the door, suit up with curiosity, and pick up a willingness to uncover the truth.

Pre-Autopsy Exercise

Before we turn up the lights and pull out the scalpel, let's start with a general external examination. Answer this question: Why did you get married?

Read the following answers and check as many reasons as apply, even if it's embarrassing to admit to some of them.

- ☐ To be more respectable
- ☐ To keep the competition away from my partner
- ☐ To create stability for my child(ren)
- ☐ To legitimize my pregnancy
- ☐ To make it harder to break up
- ☐ To make my partner a legal family member
- ☐ To become a legal member of my spouse's family
- ☐ To create long-term, shared purpose
- ☐ To act as a respectable role model for my child(ren)
- ☐ To have financial security
- ☐ To have sex without guilt
- ☐ To acquire marital benefits such as health insurance, social security, and taxes
- ☐ To prove I have a successful life
- ☐ To feel happy and fulfilled
- ☐ To avoid loneliness
- ☐ To support my spouse's wish to get married

☐ To make my parents happy

☐ To make my partner's parents happy

☐ To cut the costs of living alone

☐ To honor my faith

☐ To show the depth of my love

☐ To beat my biological clock

What did you discover about your reasons for getting married?

____

____

____

Have any of these reasons changed over time? For instance, some people get married to please their parents but later find their love grows stronger as they spend more time together. Do your reasons for marrying still make sense to you? Do your reasons for marrying affect the way you respond to your partner now?

Augustina got married to avoid loneliness. She couldn't stand being by herself in the house. Every sound was an intruder, every shadow an attacker moving closer. Her husband, Bear, was a hunter with a cache of sporting weapons—guns, bows and arrows, and knives of all shapes and sizes. Bear made her feel loved and protected. The marriage felt like a match made in heaven. When Bear decided to move out, Augustina felt alone and afraid again, so naturally she kept turning to the man who had always chased away the fear. The reason could just as well have been financial. Augustina could have married for security and held on because she didn't make enough money.

Knowing why you got married may offer powerful insight into why you're struggling to resuscitate a lifeless marriage. It could be that one or both of you have outgrown the original reason for marrying. If you find you married for the "wrong" reasons, or are holding on for the wrong reasons, use that knowledge to guide your actions now. And don't beat yourself up about it. A decision made by an eighteen-year-old can be very different from one made by a thirty-eight-year-old.

> *Insurance companies establish policies based on research that shows the human brain is not fully developed until the mid-twenties. That's why driver's insurance rates drop when a motorist reaches the age of twenty-five. The science behind this is well-established, and yet many of us make lifelong and life-altering decisions in our late teens and early twenties. Is it any wonder we have a tendency to change our minds as our brains continue to mature?*

Two Experiences, Same Cave

Two monks walk into a cave. The first monk had never left the hermitage. The second monk had traveled the world before entering the monastery. The first monk walked deep into the cave and said, "It's too dark in here. Let's keep looking." The second monk replied, "Turn around."

Just like the first monk, if you have limited experience, your perspective can be limited. You may have grown up with parents who cherished financial security because they grew up with no money, or they may have raised you with a strict moral code that encouraged marriage as a means to success, respectability, or a show of religious faith. Maybe you were shy and didn't date very often or had to move out of the house at an early age. There are so many influences that affect our choices in life, but we don't see them until we look back. By examining the events you experienced early in life, it can help you see how some of your actions could have been molded by them, which can be liberating for your actions in the now. Soren Kierkegaard said, "Life can only be understood backwards; but it must be lived forwards."

Case Study: Dan Discovers Why He Married Leigh

Dan had fallen into the trap of thinking Leigh belonged to him. He saw that holding on to her wasn't working. He signed his commitment letter to leave Leigh alone so that she could choose to swim with or without him. During the marital autopsy, he answered the questions about why he married her as realistically as he could.

Dan forced a smile as he recounted his history.

"When we first met, I thought she'd never go out with me. I grew up alone for the most part… didn't date much. I guess you could say I'm an introvert. I was a nerd with no life except school. Leigh had friends. She had a job working as a manager at Walgreens. She had her own house. That girl had it all goin' on!"

He explained how he wanted to snatch her up before someone else did. He believed that marrying Leigh would keep her from leaving him. And then there was the loneliness before they met. Marriage meant he would never have to be alone again. Children would only add to the company. He had always wanted a family, and with Leigh's looks and obvious intelligence, he reasoned that they would have the perfect children. His parents approved and his father praised him for "snagging a catch." It felt good to please his parents. For the first time, Dan felt like a real success.

Your Marital Autopsy

It's time to pick up your scalpel and start dissecting.

Directions for the Marital Autopsy Screener: On the *left side* of the inventory below, circle the ONE answer to each statement that best describes *your* behaviors within the marriage. If you get stuck trying to decide which answer is best, try to imagine what your spouse would say about you. On the *right side*, circle the best description of your *spouse's* behaviors within the marriage. Don't ask your spouse to take the inventory, either with you or without you. YOU are answering for *both of you.*

Me	Statement	Spouse
	1. Handling of disagreements	
0	Expressed disagreement in ways that drew us closer	0
1	Expressed disagreement but respected the other's opinion	1
2	Shut down and refused to speak during disagreements	2
3	Almost always held a grudge after disagreements	3
Me	**2. Recovering from disagreements**	**Spouse**
0	Worked to make up regardless of who started the argument	0
1	Took responsibility for making up most of the time	1
2	Believed that the person who is at fault should do the making up	2
3	Expected the other person to make up regardless of who was at fault	3
Me	**3. Responsibility for marital problems**	**Spouse**
0	Always took personal responsibility for role in marital problems	0
1	Was willing to consider personal responsibility for marital problems	1
2	Often blamed the other for marital problems	2
3	Almost always blamed the other for marital problems without accepting any personal responsibility	3

Me	4. History of infidelity	Spouse
0	Never had an affair	0
1	Talked about having an affair but never acted on it	1
2	Did have an affair but worked hard to repair the marriage	2
3	Had an affair and made no effort to repair the marriage	3
Me	**5. Emotional maturity (the ability to understand and manage one's emotions)**	**Spouse**
0	Very emotionally mature	0
1	Often emotionally mature	1
2	Sometimes emotionally immature but could overcome it	2
3	Often emotionally immature (emotions ruled behavior)	3
Me	**6. Expectations for the marriage**	**Spouse**
0	Believed that marriage was going to require work and gave full effort independent of partner	0
1	Believed marriage required work and gave when partner gave	1
2	Depended on spouse to work hard on the marriage	2
3	Believed things should be easy if it's "right"	3

Me	7. Equitable distribution of responsibilities	Spouse
0	Had a flexible approach to sharing responsibilities around the house	0
1	Accepted a division of labor (mowing lawn, doing dishes, cooking meals) based on each partner's skills and interests	1
2	Avoided responsibilities in the marriage	2
3	Refused to share responsibilities in the marriage	3
Me	**8. Divorce as solution**	**Spouse**
0	Refused to consider divorce as a solution	0
1	Considered divorce sometimes but never seriously	1
2	Often considered divorce as a solution	2
3	Considered divorce as the only solution	3
Me	**9. Dedication to relationship**	**Spouse**
0	Made a clear commitment to the marriage	0
1	Rarely questioned decision to marry	1
2	Sometimes blamed spouse for pushing the marriage	2
3	Frequently blamed spouse for forcing the marriage	3

Me	10. Marriage as treatment for feelings of inadequacy	Spouse
0	Felt complete and loveable before marriage	0
1	Felt satisfied but incomplete before marriage	1
2	Felt incomplete before marriage	2
3	Felt incomplete even after marriage	3
Me	**11. Growing apart over the course of the marriage**	**Spouse**
0	Worked hard to stay connected during the marriage	0
1	Noticed growing apart after marriage and tried to correct it	1
2	Grew apart in the marriage and didn't even notice	2
3	Grew apart and resented the other for it	3
Me	**12. Value placed on sex**	**Spouse**
0	Placed value on sex in the marriage	0
1	Understood that sex was or was not important to spouse	1
2	Did not value spouse's sexual needs	2
3	Understood that sex was important and used it against spouse	3
Me	**13. Trust in partner**	**Spouse**
0	Trusted spouse without reservation	0
1	Trusted spouse with most things	1
2	Rarely ever trusted spouse	2
3	Expected to be hurt by spouse	3

Me	14. Respect toward partner	Spouse
0	Showed unconditional respect for spouse	0
1	Usually showed respect for spouse	1
2	Rarely showed respect for spouse	2
3	Openly disrespected spouse in front of others	3
Me	**15. Presenting a false self**	**Spouse**
0	Shared real self before marriage	0
1	Sometimes hid less attractive qualities before marriage	1
2	Kept character weaknesses a secret before marriage	2
3	Pretended to be a different person before marriage	3
Me	**16. Unity of purpose**	**Spouse**
0	Put relationship ahead of everything, including family	0
1	Sometimes placed child or other family member first	1
2	Mostly put children and family ahead of the relationship	2
3	Always put other people or work ahead of the relationship	3
Me	**17. Value placed on marriage**	**Spouse**
0	Knew marriage could end in divorce but not for us	0
1	Knew marriage could end in divorce; worked to prevent it	1
2	Didn't see marriage as a big deal—"just a piece of paper"	2
3	Knew from the beginning that the marriage wouldn't last	3

Me	18. Sharing finances	Spouse
0	Believed money should be managed as a team	0
1	Believed money should be managed by the person best equipped	1
2	Believed one person should primarily manage the money	2
3	Refused to share any of the finances	3
Me	**19. Control issues**	**Spouse**
0	Always balanced control in the relationship	0
1	Took turns with control in the relationship	1
2	Had difficulty giving up control in the relationship	2
3	Never shared control in the relationship	3
Me	**20. Expression of jealousy**	**Spouse**
0	Showed little jealousy and had faith in partner	0
1	Showed some occasional, manageable jealousy	1
2	Showed jealousy for little reason	2
3	Showed a toxic level of jealousy	3
Me	**21. Expression of love**	**Spouse**
0	Expressed love freely and openly toward partner	0
1	Made deliberate efforts to show love almost every day	1
2	Believed love was understood without having to show it	2
3	Believed that showing love is a sign of weakness	3

Me	22. Internet addictions	Spouse
0	Internet porn sites were never an issue	0
1	Internet porn use did occur but did not affect intimacy with spouse	1
2	Internet porn use affected intimacy with spouse	2
3	Internet porn use was excessive and damaged intimacy with spouse	3

Me	23. Parental divorce	Spouse
0	Parents were married once and forever	0
1	Parents stayed married but bickered often	1
2	Parents divorced once	2
3	Parents had multiple divorces	3

Me	24. Prior divorce	Spouse
0	This is first marriage	0
1	Married once before this marriage	1
2	Married twice before this marriage	2
3	Married three or more times before this marriage	3

Me	25. Children	Spouse
0	Agreed on how to raise the children	0
1	Didn't always agree on how to raise the children but worked as a team	1
2	Often argued about how to raise the children	2
3	Parenting was the main source of conflict	3
Me	**26. Spiritual compatibility**	**Spouse**
0	Deep religious/spiritual faith	0
1	Respectful of spouse's religion/spirituality	1
2	Showed irritation over spouse's religious/spiritual beliefs	2
3	Refused to respect spouse's religious/spiritual beliefs	3
	STOP HERE FOR SCORING	
Me	**27. Abuse during disagreements**	**Spouse**
0	Disagreed respectfully	0
1	Disagreed with occasional use of foul language	1
2	Disagreed with name calling (e.g., "Stupid jerk.")	2
3	Disagreed verbally and lashed out physically	3
Me	**28. Expression of anger**	**Spouse**
0	Expressed anger in a constructive manner	0
1	Expressed flashes of anger but quickly apologized	1
2	Used physical threats or threw things to intimidate	2
3	Choked, slapped, confined, or acted out in a physical way	3

Me	29. Drugs	Spouse
0	No drug use	0
1	Occasional recreational drug use did not interfere with marriage	1
2	Occasional drug binges that interfered with the marriage	2
3	Drug dependence that interfered with the marriage	3
Me	**30. Alcohol**	Spouse
0	No alcohol use	0
1	Occasional alcohol use did not interfere with the marriage	1
2	Alcohol binges that did interfere with the marriage	2
3	Alcohol dependence a problem that interfered with the marriage	3

Scoring and Meaning

The Marital Autopsy Screener (MAS) was developed as an informal questionnaire for individuals undergoing divorce. It is composed of items regularly cited as a cause for marital dissolution. The MAS has not been empirically validated. It is not meant to diagnose or take the place of treatment for marital problems.

Generally, items with a *score of 0 or 1* indicate issues in your relationship that are not likely a source of significant conflict. If you've scored your spouse in this range, perhaps he or she is a model partner, but first make sure your responses are not based on an idealized image of your spouse. Breakups can be like the death of a loved one, we may have a tendency to remember the good things and gloss over less endearing behaviors. If you aren't sure about the accuracy of your scoring, ask someone who knows you and your relationship well enough to review your answers. Do *not* ask your spouse. Remember this instrument is not to be shared with him or her, it is for your use only.

Items with a *score of 2* fall within the typical range of couples who suffer with relationship problems. These issues can be improved upon, but they require commitment. If the 2's are coming from your spouse's column, use the information to remember that your separation is an opportunity for change, and change is necessary. If there are some 2's in your column, how do you feel about them? Were you aware when you were engaging in these behaviors? Were you following some modeling by your parents from childhood? These are important concerns to address because they can stifle a relationship, but the good news is that most are under your control.

Items with a *score of 3* can point to major cracks in the foundation of your relationship. They are not normally correctable on your own. Active intervention in these areas is usually required before the relationship can be viable. The items with a score of 3 may very well be the cause of your separation or divorce. These problems should not be overlooked, because they are relationship killers and they can turn into serial killers for every future relationship if they are not addressed.

How to Determine a Total Score

Add up all items in the left column under "Me" to obtain the total score for yourself. Add up your spouse's score in the right column *separately* to determine your spouse's total (but remember to leave out the last four items). The scores below interpret a total for one person at a time. Remember that no single high score on an item is proof that the entire marriage was doomed.

Score 0-27: A score in this range suggests the scored person's contribution to the marital problems were not necessarily any worse than any other person who is married. Take a look at any items that scored 3 points for either yourself or your spouse. Consider the impact these 3-pointers have had on your breakup. Even though you scored within the normal range for your marriage as a whole, there may still be something to learn from the individual items you've scored in the extreme. All couples have areas of disagreement or factors from the past that can put a strain on their feelings of security.

Score 28 and above: A score at or above 28 on the MAS indicates difficulty getting along in the relationship. It is also important to look at whether there is a discrepancy between your spouse's score and your score. If one of your scores is significantly higher than the others, it is worthwhile to see what kind of impact that has had on the breakup. For example, if you have the higher score, take a look at items you scored 2 or 3 on to see if there is some contribution those behaviors had on the death of your marriage. You can use this information to help you take control of your life. Even historical items like number of previous marriages or parental marriages, while not changeable, may expose feelings of vulnerability. Regardless of scoring within this problematic range, understand that high scores do not always pinpoint the causes behind a terminal marriage. If you are feeling concerned about your own high score, consider seeking an evaluation by a qualified professional. A high score on your spouse's side of the screener does not authorize you to counsel him or her about their mistakes or how to fix them. No one likes to hear "I told you so!"

The Toxic Four: The last 4 items on the MAS include specific references to Verbal Abuse, Physical Abuse, Drugs and Alcohol. These items are not included in the total score because they can destroy any relationship. These items must be isolated and considered toxic for any marriage until proven otherwise. In medicine, we say a new onset seizure is a brain tumor until proven otherwise. That's because seizures typically start in childhood so having a fit for the first time after age 40 is due to a brain tumor until new information proves us wrong. Similarly, we can't say that all abuse leads to divorce, but if divorce occurs in a marriage where there is abuse, it is likely that the abuse killed the marriage until proven otherwise. It is important to consider the frequency and the context of these behaviors to help you realize the risk they represent. For example, both verbal and physical abuse in the context of the loss of control that can occur with drug or alcohol abuse can quickly turn deadly. That doesn't mean that fewer or less frequent behaviors aren't as dangerous, which means all of these items must be considered with great deliberation. Regardless of your total score on the MAS, if you have answered 2 or more on any of the last 4 items for either you or your spouse, consider seeking help from a professional who can guide you through the lingering effects of these relationship toxins.

Review your responses

Each item in the inventory relates to issues that are typically listed by couples as reasons for divorce. Did you see specific areas you know you could work on to create a better marriage? If yes, what are they?

____

____

____

What did you learn about your spouse or the things that made you feel unhappy in the marriage? It's okay to acknowledge them. Everything we discuss here is for your use only.

____

____

____

Is there something you needed from your spouse that you weren't getting? If so, what?

____

____

____

Is there something you think you could have been doing to help your relationship that you couldn't bring yourself to do? What is it, and why couldn't you do it?

____

____

____

Case Study: Dan's Autopsy Results

Dan unraveled the survey he'd wadded up into a ball the night before. His answers had pinned down some of the gremlins in his marriage, and he wasn't happy about it. On his questionnaire, he acknowledged a brief affair with a coworker a year earlier. Although he had worked hard to make it up to his wife, seeing it circled on paper in black and white added weight to his loss. He was seeing it now through Leigh's eyes, and the pain was sharp.

Several months back, when he had first told Leigh about the affair, she threw him out of the house. Weeks later when she was ready to talk about it, Dan felt ashamed and shut down the conversation. He refused to get into specifics.

"Why keep stirring that bucket of sh-t?" he insisted.

Leigh kept pressing, and he overreacted, throwing a glass against the wall. Several apologies and edible arrangements later, he was still in the doghouse. Dan remembered feeling irritated because Leigh kept nursing her suspicions. No matter how hard he tried to make things right, she couldn't forgive and forget, and he resented her for not letting it go.

According to Dan: "She'd get mad at everyday stuff, and she definitely didn't want sex with me anymore." Leigh had lost trust in him, growing more distant. When he called to say he had to work late, something he'd done for years before, her voice turned ice cold. She couldn't recapture the love she once had for him. And her resentments were building too. Not just for his affair, but for her inability to get promoted because of Dan's military moves and for her life alone with the kids during his deployments. Their marital upsets stopped feeling like the occasional pops of grease from a hot frying pan. The fire of discontent had raged out of control with flames so high, it set off alarm bells that Leigh heard as a signal to escape with their two girls. Divorce was the only option that made sense to her.

In therapy, Dan had described a time before Leigh left when the relationship got better. It happened when she asked him to go to church as a family.

"But I just couldn't keep it up. She wanted me to go every single Sunday." He made excuses and eventually stopped going. He wasn't much of a believer. He was only doing it to please Leigh.

"She kept telling me that I needed to go with her, that we weren't equally yoked. I said, 'What are we, some kind of farm animals?'"

Joking about her faith only made things worse. Looking back, he realized he'd missed an important opportunity to rebuild their relationship by sharing in her faith. It was very likely the thing that would have helped her to forgive him. He didn't realize Leigh was depending on her spiritual beliefs to get over her feelings of betrayal, to convince herself to give their marriage a second chance. Both Dan and Leigh came from families of divorce, and it clouded their beliefs about the odds of staying together in the first place.

Reviewing the autopsy was hard for Dan. But the effect was glaring. It shined a light on his behaviors in a way that made him realize he had played a major part in Leigh's decision to leave. Now, instead of blaming her for tearing the family apart, he could see that each of them had driven a spear into the wounds of their dying marriage. Dan had hoped his brief affair would be an ugly but brief blip on the screen, not realizing how long it takes to recover from a breach of trust.

On the other hand, Leigh was taking on a type of martyr role, surrendering her career and her independence to support Dan's military position. The kids kept her busy after work so that by nighttime, she was too exhausted to make love. She felt hurt by his affair but didn't understand how rejected Dan felt when he reached out for her in the night. After learning of his infidelity, she couldn't clearly express what she needed from him. Turning the other cheek proved too great a stretch despite her faith. Both Dan and Leigh had lost their desire to keep laboring at the work of loving, but as fate would have it, they dropped their shovels at different times.

Completing this exercise helped Dan understand Leigh's decision to leave. He still believed they could work things out, but seeing his part in the breakup gave him the insight he needed to remain patient. He worked hard to avoid those impulsive phone calls to talk Leigh into coming back.

"I'm starting to figure it out. I need to give her the time I wish she'd given me when I screwed up."

Go back over your answers and see which areas you scored high on and which your spouse scored high on. Is there any balancing of scales here, or is it clear that one of you was creating more pain for the other? The answers will help you navigate better as we move along to the next chapters.

If something specific in the survey strikes you as particularly important or rocks your understanding of your marriage, share your insight with a friend, a minister, or a therapist. Do not talk to your ex about it. It is a difficult temptation to resist but keep working on your commitment to your growth. Make believe you're playing a card game and keep your aces close to the vest for the time being. There will be plenty of time to share with them later, if you both choose.

Exercise: Autopsy Report

Using the results from the autopsy inventory and the list of reasons you got married, write down the top three issues that contributed to the death of your relationship. Be sure to include at least one issue that was based on your own behavior, even if it is something like your difficulty leaving an abusive relationship or one marred by addiction. This is not victim blaming. It is a search for truth that transcends reproach to reach greater understanding.

1. Top Three Relationship Toxins

a) ________________________________

b) ________________________________

c) ________________________________

2. In what specific ways can you use the image of your dead marriage as inspiration for changing your reactions to your spouse?

Example: *I realize I married to feel more emotionally secure. Now that I think of my marriage as dead, I can focus on finding my own security in my new life.*

____

____

____

It took courage for you to stand under the hot autopsy room lights and assess the damage. Can you feel it? Hopefully, you've learned something about the toxic beliefs and behaviors that killed your relationship. From here on, we will only refer to your spouse as your "ex" It will help you to remember that the old relationship you knew is over. Think of it as a type of transformation, like when a baby bird first discovers it can fly after a lifetime of living in the nest. You're growing stronger by your labor. You're ready to move on to the next section, but this is still the beginning. Let's move out of the morgue and rejoin the world of the living.

Chapter Five Lessons:

- ☯ The end of a relationship is rarely one person's doing
- ☯ Don't believe every thought your mind lobs at you
- ☯ The old relationship is dead. A marriage cannot survive without two committed people
- ☯ Most faiths see death as a means to new life

Chapter 6.

I'd rather live in a shack than face another day with that woman. —*Jeff, securities analyst*

Have you looked at your ex lately and wondered how they became Mr. Hyde without drinking a potion? Some common descriptors are: *insane ... horrible ... selfish ... coward ... bloodsucker.* And those are just the ones we can print for a general audience! You married a good person, right? How could they be acting so badly? Understanding the potential reasons for their alien behaviors may help you build compassion for the struggle your ex is facing and the impact of those behaviors on you.

Before we examine the Leavers' profiles, a note of caution is in order. We are complicated beings. One individual is never as neat and tidy as a profile might suggest and there are many motivations for a spouse to leave. Value judgments about whether the reasons are good or bad might feel satisfying in the moment, but don't pin that scarlet letter on their chest just yet. The snapshots in this chapter were created as a guide to steady your nerves, not as a mugshot for criticism. Understanding the reasons behind a Leaver's behavior can guide your decisions about how to respond while helping you steer clear of accusations.

Profile: The Life Force Seeker

Life Force Seekers (LFSs) believe they're losing their youthful vitality. They look in the mirror and see an expanding waistline or gray, thinning hair. When they go outside they may notice there's no one checking them out anymore. Their youth feels like a distant memory, with happy days in the rearview mirror and nothing but dark clouds up ahead.

Sometimes, but not always, the LFS finds a younger lover to regain their balance. Like the distinctive call of a domestic bird, LFS's have a native call:

"There's gotta be more to life."

"She [the new lover] makes me feel love… passion… young… alive… happy."

"You don't excite me anymore." An LFS may have put off pleasure to meet obligations, career goals, or family expectations. The longer they've put off their passions, the harder the crash. These individuals eventually take a hard look at life and feel desperate. Their behaviors can be just as desperate: cheating, drinking, drugging, spending ... and quitting. So what if they have a well-paying job, a loving family, and security? That's not the point. They want to feel alive, to look attractive, to be desired. They want to shout out like Dylan Thomas: "Do not go gentle into that good night but rage, rage against the dying of the light."

Many LFSs have affairs with people who are younger and full of vitality. Their choices are about feeling potent—not just sexually, but full of potential. They're looking for a life force that will break them out of their "forced" life.

We've all seen the middle-aged man with the stereotypical convertible, wearing a speedo, and spending money to look younger. Nothing will stop them from seeking the Force, not even their aging biology. According to a report by Grand View Research Inc., the market for erectile dysfunction drugs like Viagra, Cialis and Levitra is expected to reach 3.2 billion dollars by 2022.

Erik Erikson, a psychologist famous for his theories of psychosocial development, described nine stages of life that present challenges to our mental and emotional growth. We can either move through these stage or get bogged down by the challenges they create. The closest description for the LFS stage is found in what Erikson called "Generativity versus Stagnation." The LFS has hit a brick wall of "stagnation," and they are desperate to hit the gas and crash through to the other side where life feels good again. The bricks are heavy with the challenge of aging. They've lost sight of the big picture, of the wisdom we gain over the years. Instead, they remain stuck in immediate gratification through hedonistic desires which can involve the basic instinct of mating. As a result, the LFS may put the needs of the family aside to seek satisfaction. They follow an Epicurean philosophy of: "Eat, drink, and be merry, for tomorrow we die."

It helps to remember that the driving force behind the LFS's decisions is fear. Mostly they fear growing old and losing their place in society as a force to be reckoned with. Allowing yourself to understand the LFS's fears can take the sting out of the rejection they serve up as they flip through old recipes for happiness.

Case Study: Ted and the Clash

Ted was married to Adela, a retired schoolteacher. They had a wonderful life. He was successful in his career as an airline pilot. Adela was drawing retirement from teaching. The kids were getting ready to leave the house, opening a long-awaited gate to freedom and travel. One son was a senior in high school, and the other had just left for college.

"It was supposed to be our time together," explained Ted.

Instead of living out their South American backpacking plans, Adela told Ted that she wanted a divorce. She had already picked out an apartment and put down a deposit. Ted was shocked.

"She's working out every day and dressing like some kind of punk rock star. She's even got a nose ring. God knows what else she's pierced!" He described something else he never thought his wife was capable of doing: "Adela has given up on the kids. Last time we were together, she told me, 'They're gone. They don't need me anymore.' She even has a boyfriend now."

Her behavior seemed totally irrational to him.

"Why would a woman give up the dreams we worked all our lives for to go partying with Evel Knievel. He's fourteen years younger and rides a Harley!"

In divorce group, we discussed LFS behaviors, suggesting that his wife might be afraid of aging and the prejudice of becoming "a little old lady."

The tattoos, daily workouts, and new clothes might be her way of grabbing youth by its punk rock Mohawk. To his dismay, Ted discovered that standing in judgment and trying to change her mind only made things worse. Adela didn't want anyone telling her what to do. She wanted to feel free. In her mind, Ted was pulling her down under the water and she was already fighting some rough waves. Losing her role as an active mom and facing the pain of an empty nest when the youngest planned to leave for college was too much to handle.

Ted did his best to cope with her decision to move to a different part of town. He focused on the moment, one heart beat at a time, despite wanting her to keep her promise to stay forever. Traveling alone was never part of the plan.

Once, while out with friends, he saw Adela with her boyfriend at the bar. They were kissing with abandon, and it made him sick.

"I was there with our friends. Both our friends until she dumped them… dumped all of us."

The tears rolled down his face as he continued.

"She was leaning against the bar. He was kissing all over her, and she was laughing so loud, we could all hear it. I just had to get out of there. I paid for my meal and left without eating a bite. Why did she have to do that in our place… the place we'd eat chicken wings and cheeseburgers as a family?"

It took time for Ted to realize that he was not responsible for Adela's behavior. He struggled to accept the reality that she no longer dreamed of the future he had in mind: "Talking sense" sounded more like nonsense to Adela. Ted learned the hard way that assuming the role of adult made him a parent and marked him as the enemy, someone to rebel against.

Erikson's theory of midlife struggles would suggest that the LFS stage occurs in our forties and later, but there is research suggesting that it can happen sooner in life, as early as the thirties. Also, the stereotype of the aging man driving the convertible is changing. As we have seen with Adela, many women are leaving their marriages for the same reason and with increasing frequency.

Profile: The Long-Suffering Martyr

At first glance, the Long-Suffering Martyr (LSM) looks like the opposite of the Life Force Seeker. Instead of focusing on regaining their happy youth, this departing spouse targets their history of suffering. Typically, the LSM has put off their needs to take care of others, especially family. They are fed up, and believe that happiness is just around the corner, out of sight of their marriage. This ex eyes their spouse and sees a selfish user. If they have played a submissive role in their relationship, they will fear being stepped on again in the future, so they fling the doormat life out the window as a way to take charge.

The LSM says things like:

"I give and give, and all you do is take and take."

"I'm not going to let you use me anymore."

"It's my turn."

"I don't need to change—you do."

The LSM seems to enjoy inflicting emotional pain on their spouse because it is fair punishment for their anger and disappointment. If the LSM sees you crying over the breakup, they might say, "Good! Now you know what it feels like." Resentment has built up after unmet expectations that their mate would see their sacrifice and shower them with appreciation. When the gratitude is absent or insufficient, they are likely to complain to a friend or family member instead of addressing their dissatisfaction directly with their partner. The LSM isn't ready to see their part in the relationship conflict or in allowing their needs to go unmet for so long that escaping the marriage seems the only solution. They believe that their spouse is not capable of meeting their needs. Stuck in a cycle of giving without the rewards they seek, the LSM will suffer silently or lash out in anger. Instead of building assertiveness and seeking a solution from within the marriage, they believe it is better to walk away and start over. They're likely to justify their departure as "the right thing" by weaving events into a story of unrequited servitude. As evidenced in the name, the LSM has suffered for a long time, at least months, if not years. The chronicity of unhappiness can lead to depression and anxiety which can complicate their ability to recover from lack of assertiveness and self-care.

Case Study: Sam, Sam, the LSM

Sam was a good example of a Long-Suffering Martyr. He'd given up his career so his wife, Beth, could join the military as an officer. He took care of the kids while she worked long hours and took off for deployments overseas as a combat nurse. She was preparing for a deployment to Afghanistan when Sam told her, "You can't go because I'm the one leaving this time. It's my turn."

The news came as a huge blow to Beth. She had worked hard and volunteered for risky deployments to advance her career. In her mind, she was doing it for the good of the family. How could Sam end the marriage knowing how much she loved and needed him? They had two children and he was the stay-at-home dad. The idea of Sam walking out on her and the children was like a doctor leaving his crowded clinic without warning. She thought they had a good marriage. Yes, they argued from time to time. She remembered one time when he had complained to Beth's mother that he wasn't a priority, but she reasoned that he was just venting and that all couples had their ups and downs. He had to know how much she loved him. Why else would she be working so hard to provide for the family?

In divorce group, she lamented, "He was always so helpful, so responsible. I could always count on him."

Beth couldn't accept Sam's decision to leave.

"All I ever did was work to keep us afloat, and now he says I was only doing it for me… that I never cared about him."

The more she tried to convince him to change his mind, the more he blamed her. She began to doubt herself.

"Did I do it all wrong? If I was so bad for so many years, why didn't he say anything about it before?" In her clearer moments, she realized he had commented about her absences when the stress at work and home built up. He told her he needed her to stay home with him, to "let someone else deploy, to take their turn in the sandbox." But she hadn't taken his complaints seriously because she knew how important he was to her and the kids: "Why couldn't he understand that?"

Beth felt miserable. When she tried to approach the subject of her grief over losing him, Sam doubled down: "You see! This is exactly what I'm talking about. You only care about yourself, how you're hurt. What I've done to *you.* I told you what I needed, but you never listened because you only care about yourself!"

Beth was in a no-win situation. If she brought up all the things she'd done to support him, he would turn it back on her selfishness for not seeing his side. If she asked him what she could do differently, he'd say that it didn't matter anymore. It was "too little, too late."

Sam was playing the role of the martyr. He saw himself as the victim in the marriage, and his wife had to be the villain for it to work. Over time, Beth came to realize that Sam had a hard time asking for what he wanted in general, not just from her.

By blaming and leaving, LSMs don't have to work to make things better. In their minds, they've done all the heavy lifting, and now they're ready to drop the entire load. For all their arguing about not getting what they need, there is a more pernicious fear-- that they are not valuable. Rather than hold on and fight for their right to be loved as they want, the LSM chooses to escape. They leave in search of a new life, or a new love, hoping their needs will come first the next time around.

Profile: The Uncertain Spouse

Uncertain spouses (US) aren't sure whether to stay or go. Their behavior changes like Ginger Rogers following Fred Astaire's steps—always maintaining a precise distance apart. When the emotional scales of the relationship tip too far in either direction, the US shifts their weight to regain balance. If their spouse pulls away, they find a reason to visit or spend more time together. If the spouse moves in too close, they bolt to create more distance. Like a two-year-old, they want to feel independent and explore the world but can only tolerate a certain distance away from Mommy or Daddy. You can suspect you're dealing with a US when you hear words like:

"I think we should separate for a while… I need space."

"I know I said we should separate, but I never said you could date."

"Where have you been all weekend?"

Because the US's ambivalence pulls them in opposite directions, it creates a degree of unpredictability that strangles intimacy and trust. Their spouse is constantly on pins and needles, afraid to say or do the wrong thing that will send their US fleeing in the opposite direction. The relationship can die slowly from a "thousand cuts," with frequent threats of the final break up. Over time, the relationship becomes more of an emotional roller coaster ride than a functioning relationship. The result is lots of tiptoeing by the partner met by fake certainty on the part of the US who actually suffers from ambivalence rather than conviction.

Case Study: US against Bob

Jennifer told Bob she wasn't in love with him anymore. Next, she asked him to move out. It broke his heart, but he found a cheap apartment, while she remained in the home with their two pre-school children. When Bob called home to check in, Jen complained that he was pestering her and not giving her the space she needed. When he didn't call, she'd question him about his activities, like a detective interrogating a criminal.

"Where were you last night? Who did you go out with? Did you even think about calling your kids?"

Jennifer could only tolerate so much distance or closeness before taking action. As you might imagine, the push-pull made Bob feel like an emotional yo-yo.

"One minute she wants me around, and the next she's telling me I'm suffocating her."

Jennifer's uncertainty revolved around her insecurity about life outside of her marriage. Having her husband available meant she could take chances, knowing he would step in if things got bad. When she took those chances, new and exciting things happened. She'd meet new people, learn new skills, or discover dormant talents. She'd enjoy breaking out of the cocoon of her relationship and finding independence, but then the wheel would spin again and her emancipation would feel too risky. The pipes in her kitchen would leak and she'd feel helpless again. Or Bob would stay away and she worried he was happier without her. She didn't entertain the possibility of being more independent within her marriage because it would mean committing to a future together. In her mind, she was either stuck and married or single and free. She wasn't ready to take a side, and the middle ground was swallowing her up like the San Andreas fault.

Bob learned to accept the ambivalence Jennifer was feeling by noticing the actions that determined her behavior. He even had some fun taking on the role of fortuneteller. "I could predict that if I stopped calling on any given week, she'd text me before Sunday. So I purposely held off, and BINGO! Here comes the text from Jen like clockwork." After a few months, Bob wasn't having fun anymore because her behavior was growing more irrational and unpredictable. He began the work of restoring his life independent of Jennifer's reactions and made plans on his own without looking for an effect. He trusted that his life would get better if he stopped trying to force an outcome.

Dan, our story's hero, was married to a blend of profiles. Before they met, Leigh had close friends who liked to go out after work. She enjoyed dancing at clubs, smoking pot, and drinking shots to unwind. When she married Dan and had children, everything changed. She worked hard to be a role model for the kids. Dan worked long hours, so it was tough to count on him for a break. During some of their late-night talks, after the kids were in bed, she'd drink and say how she really felt.

"This isn't me. I don't want to be the supermom. I don't think I was meant to have kids."

Dan heard the alcohol talking and stored his loving wife in the soft spot in his heart where his family lived. In his mind, Leigh was a great mother with little time for much else, including sex. It stung when she rejected him, but he'd turn on the TV and watch movies until his lids got heavy with sleep. Leigh wasn't avoiding sex because she was overextended; after two children, and no time off from work, she had gained 40 pounds and felt disgusted with her body. Gravity and breastfeeding had transformed her mirror into an enemy. When she started a New Year's resolution to do something about her weight, Dan was too busy to support her exercise schedule. Reluctant to pester him, and victim to her flagging excitement, Leigh gave up asking for help and gave in to helplessness.

When she left him, her goal was to rediscover the fun person she had once been. When Dan tried to help, it was too little too late for her. Leigh's future was uncertain, but getting rid of Dan would set her on the right path. Later, we'll see how Dan's behaviors changed her reactions within their relationship. Social scientists tell us that no one can control another person's actions, but the law of physics teaches us that for every action there is an equal and opposite reaction. We'll see how this paradox played out in Dan and Leigh's marriage as he made changes in his life.

Exercise: Staying Balanced

Don't be surprised if your ex shows up in more than one profile—there is plenty of room for overlap across all of the reasons for leaving. We know that in each case, whether it's the LFS, LSM, US, or something else, the best course of action is to avoid rescue. That means it's best not to try to change your ex's mind in order to save them from lapses in judgment. The logical part of your brain probably knows this already. But what is it that prevents you from detaching? Take a look at the list below and check any feelings that apply. Don't be embarrassed if you check them all; each can be a normal reaction to a spouse who leaves:

- ☐ Abandonment
- ☐ Loneliness
- ☐ Desire for revenge
- ☐ Outrage
- ☐ Betrayal
- ☐ Fear of the unknown
- ☐ Worry

☐ Panic

☐ Hatred

☐ Sorrow

☐ Grief

☐ Guilt

☐ Resentment

☐ Frustration

☐ Hope

☐ Commitment

It's easy to brush all this profile stuff aside and drop back to blaming your ex. After all, they made a promise, right? A promise is forever. Your mind is capable of understanding that people change. A promise is based on an ideal and many people fall short of ideals despite their promises. But your emotions are instinctual—they aren't based on reason. You may find yourself in a struggle between your logic, telling you to give your ex some space, and your urge to lash out, cajole, threaten, or punish. Later on, we'll be teaching you how to use Wise Mind to help you to negotiate peace between your warring logic and emotions. For now, let's try to understand how the battle is affecting your behavior.

Based on the feelings you checked above, how are you reacting to your ex? Check all the actions you may be taking in reaction to your emotions.

☐ Begging for a second chance

☐ Limiting time with the kids

☐ Creating jealousy

☐ Withholding money

☐ Cursing

- ☐ Slamming or throwing things
- ☐ Blaming
- ☐ Acting possessive
- ☐ Reminding your ex about the promise to stay forever
- ☐ Physically barring your ex's exit from the home
- ☐ Calling the "other" man/woman to make them go away
- ☐ Threatening to call the boss or family

We've identified common divorce emotions followed by fruitless behaviors to prove a point: your emotions do not define you, but your actions could. You have a right to your feelings, but you do not have a right to hurt others based on your feelings. By controlling your actions when *inter*acting with your ex, you will be in control of 50% of each exchange.

Your ex's transformation from the good spouse to "Dread Lord Evil" might seem to have happened overnight, but it's not a case of being good or bad, these labels are just shortcuts that lead you away from a deeper understanding of their motivations. By now the autopsy and Leaver profiles have shown you that there were warning signs before the final break—signs like job burnout, stress, depression, irritability, increased arguments, avoidance of intimacy within the marriage or increased intimacy with others.

Even after learning about the profiles, many members of our divorce group have asked how could he or she be so cold. It's a valid question. How is it that the Leaver, regardless of profile, can appear so unfeeling or unwilling to bend?

The best way to understand the sudden detachment is to look at the months leading up to the separation. Most departing spouses have made the decision to leave months if not years before they walk out the door. They've already gone through much of the internal debate and soul-searching. By the time they announce their decision, it's down to a question of how (not whether) to put their exit strategy into practice.

> *PEARL: The departing spouse has usually made the decision to leave long before going.*

The announcement of the separation may have come as a huge blow to you, but your ex has already had time to think about it and to plan, even if they appear to have locked into the decision overnight. You may see little emotion, but that doesn't mean they don't have feelings for you. What does matter is that the mental and emotional preparation you've had is probably minimal in comparison to their prep time. The scales are not balanced yet, so give yourself permission to grieve and to catch up.

Chapter Six Lessons:

- ☯ Promises are built on the expectation of permanence but life is rooted in change
- ☯ Your emotions do not define you but your actions can
- ☯ Labelling your ex as "bad" hides a deeper understanding of their motivations
- ☯ Give yourself permission to grieve and catch up with the changes in your life

Chapter 7. Climbing the Spiral Staircase

It feels more like loneliness than grief.
—Sandra G., college professor

You've just finished reading about why Leaver's leave. You deserve equal time. Your emotions may be steeped in grief and mourning. But why? No one has died. The answer lies in one word—attachment.

The pain of losing your ex is directly proportional to the strength of your attachment. You feel restless but have nowhere to go. Like an elephant sitting on your chest, the attachment feels so heavy, it keeps you stuck in place, staring into a dark grey future. Life doesn't feel real. Even the beauty of a spectacular sunrise loses the power to amaze because it reminds you that your "other half" isn't there to share it with you.

The physical upset during a breakup is very real. I've met some of my patients for the first time in an emergency room because they swore their chest pain was a heart attack. Once the EKG results show their heart is normal, the diagnosis of panic attack takes center stage. Exit ER doctor stage left. Cue the psychologist to enter stage right. ER doctors bow out rather quickly once they decide the symptoms are "supratentorial", medical jargon for "it's all in their head." While it's true that panic won't kill you, the feeling of impending doom is terrifying and needs fast attention.

Do you feel tightness in your throat, as if you're on the verge of tears? Have you been sighing more lately? According to researchers at the University of Leuven in Belgium, sighing is nature's equivalent of a mental reset. It's a regulatory response when our breathing pattern has become abnormal for too long. If your breathing is too fast and shallow for too long, it can change your blood's pH level. Even a small change in pH can trigger panic. A sigh seems to be nature's way of rebooting the breathing system—our body's way of correcting an imbalance.

Are you finding it hard to keep food down? Maybe you have no appetite at all. The "divorce diet" is the only diet that offers weight loss with no effort. Nighttime brings on a whole new battle. You feel exhausted but can't sleep. When you do fall asleep, the peace of that brief anesthesia doesn't last. And then there are the dreams about your ex. Some dreams are comforting, like the ones where you're making love or reliving some happy time together. Other dreams are flat out nightmares where you're lashing out while under attack. No matter the content, your dreams are a window into your attachment. It helps to pay attention to the themes or actions that are occurring in your dreams. Journaling can help. Use your writing to document your reactions. You'll be amazed at how much you will grow over the next few weeks.

Post-Traumatic Stress

Post-traumatic stress is a normal reaction to an abnormal situation like war or rape, but divorce can be traumatic and just as emotionally painful. Irritability or rage, emotional numbing, high anxiety, and avoidance of people and places are defining features of post-traumatic stress. The reaction can turn into a disorder (PTSD) but that doesn't happen as often as you might think. For some people, trauma transforms their thinking in a positive way, creating post-traumatic growth. The trauma itself is the trigger, but exposure to a horrific event isn't a straight-jacket, it can be harnessed to free the spirit and promote resilience. That's why, on average, only about 25% of people who are exposed to trauma go on to develop PTSD. That means that for about 75% of victims, the impact is either neutral or an opportunity to rise from the ashes.

Post-traumatic growth depends on how we frame our hardship. Victor Frankl, a famous psychiatrist and philosopher who survived the horrors of a concentration camp, offered a human face to disaster and post-traumatic growth. His award-winning book, *Man's Search for Meaning*, explores the way we create meaning and purpose in the face of adversity. Frankl famously wrote, "When we are no longer able to change a situation, we are challenged to change ourselves."

Post-traumatic growth doesn't mean you don't hurt; pain is critical to healing. But by forcing you out of your familiar space, your partner (whether they know it or not) has challenged you to grow. You can respond by caving in, or like Dr. Frankl, you can discover meaning through your struggle.

Stages of Grief

It's hard to explain loss without referring to Elizabeth Kübler Ross's stages of grief. In her capacity as a doctor, Kübler Ross interviewed terminal patients to understand what they needed beyond prescriptions and "stiff upper lip" encouragements. Before her book *On Death and Dying* was published, terminal patients were the Siberian prisoners of the medical world, banished to remote wards, far away from treatable patients. Rather than ignore the incurable, Kübler Ross leaned in closer and listened. She heard the anguish of the dying as well as the joys. In return, these patients rewarded her with a deeper understanding of the universality of loss. She summarized their grief in five stages:

1) denial
2) bargaining
3) depression
4) anger
5) acceptance.

Those who came after her, adapted the stages to other types of grief like: divorce, military trauma and the empty nest, but some critical information was omitted along the way.

- ☯ We think of the stages as clear-cut, with a beginning, middle and end. They aren't.
- ☯ We assume the stages are the same regardless of the type of loss, but they can and do look different depending on the source of grief.

After learning about the five stages, most grievers take them literally, planning their recovery from denial to the other side using the shortest distance between two points: "I made it past denial and bargaining. Now, if I can just zip through depression, and anger, I'll cross the finish line into acceptance. Once I reach acceptance, I'll feel normal again." They rev up their engines, set their GPS to acceptance, and shift their mental gear into overdrive. There's just one problem: if somehow they manage to reach acceptance, a few days later they are feeling angry and depressed all over again. The stages of grief are not linear. You don't start at denial and end at acceptance, never to cry again.

Instead of thinking of your loss as a straight-line on the road to acceptance, imagine a spiral staircase. The spirals take you through a full 360 degrees, in repeating revolutions of denial, bargaining, anger, depression and acceptance.

> *PEARL: Grief is a spiral staircase, not a straight line.*

"I thought I'd reached acceptance. How can I be bargaining again?"

It's because emotions are complicated—they don't follow a straight-line, and they resist being ruled. The good news is that once you've tasted acceptance, it's a lot easier to savor it again. More good news! Once you've been through them a few times, you don't stay in the early stages as long. You can even shortcut the anger and sadness if you don't make those emotions your enemy. More on that when we explore Radical Acceptance. For now, let's take a look at the different stages of grief.

Denial

The term "denial" is a favorite in our culture. Most people can tell you that "denial" is an unwillingness to face the truth. When a loved one dies, it's common for friends and family to feel shocked, refusing to believe it happened. But what does denial look like when the person is still alive?

Divorce is like death without the closure. It's the food addict who envies the recovering alcoholic for not drinking, when they must eat to live. I've heard patients say they would rather have their spouse dead than live with the slow-drip torture of their ex "always out there, just a phone call away." Here are some words of denial:

"This can't be happening."

"I won't let it happen."

"He'll never go through with it."

"She'll be back."

"It's just a phase."

Notice that these words suggest an attachment to the outcome of keeping the marriage. Losing a partner is so frightening that the fear can keep you locked in an unhealthy relationship.

As humans, we have a natural tendency to survive. If we see a shark in the water, we swim for safety. If our door flies open on a dark and stormy night, we shut and lock it. Danger gets our attention. Our nervous system floods our bloodstream with adrenaline in response to fearful things. The fight or flight reaction competes with logic because fear happens in the primitive brain, while reason takes place in the hinterlands of the frontal lobe. Think of fear as a Lamborghini on a superhighway and reason as a John Deere tractor working its way up a neural backroad. That is why you feel fear in milliseconds, but it takes a few seconds to figure out a math problem. The desperation to save your marriage can overload your senses the same as a burglar invading your home. And therein lies the rub, you can lock out a burglar and call the police but you can't lock out your fear of losing your marriage.

Denial is a tricky thing; sometimes it can even sound like relief. Notice how the statements below can appear life-affirming, but like classic denial, they conceal an unconscious wish to avoid grief. It's like trying to buy a pain-free pass to happiness… sounds great in theory, but it doesn't happen in real life.

"Good riddance."

"I'm better off without him."

"Now I can date again."

"I'm free ... no more ball and chain."

"Par-ta-a-ay!"

These declarations sound powerful and invigorating, but when they surface at the beginning of the grief process, they are a smokescreen concealing denial. If you weren't seeking the divorce in the first place, why would you suddenly be so happy to end the marriage? It is entirely possible that your ex simply had the nerve to do what you've been planning all along, but that's not the norm. The statements of denial above are about as real as your nocturnal dreams. If you're not sure whether your happiness is denial in disguise, don't worry. Reality, like an alarm clock, has a way of jarring us awake.

There is another kind of denial that occurs during divorce that Kübler-Ross's model doesn't address because her data was based on the dying, not the divorcing. The Leaver's pain. We refuse to accept that our ex is feeling pain, especially when they say, "I'm not in love with you," or "I'm in love with someone else." The natural reaction for the person who is being left, is to lash out.

"I hate you!"

It is rare to see a loving response in the early stages of divorce because society teaches us that our spouse belongs to us "until death do us part." We feel protected beneath the cloak of our vows; it's the promise that protects us from abandonment: "He made a promise to be faithful, and by God, he should keep that promise. I don't have to release him, and I surely don't have to feel sorry for him!" In this way, marriage falls short of reflecting God's love, or what the Greeks called "agape" love. Agape love is not romantic or erotic love; it is the purest form of love insofar as it transcends the physical to become a selfless valuing of the other. Agape love does not seek to possess. Like a tree that offers shade to both the nature lover and the lumberjack, Agape is the highest form of unconditional love. Accepting the Leaver's pain without ulterior motives is an expression of Agape love that few of us are capable of realizing.

Bargaining

Family members of the terminally ill try to bargain for a loved one's recovery. They try to cut a deal with God or the Universe by making promises of personal sacrifice, like giving up cigarettes or feeding the hungry in return for their loved one's healing. Offerings are also made during divorce, but most of the bargaining is done directly with the departing spouse. The griever comes up with all the enticing offers they can think of, firing off a barrage of enticements, hoping to find a chink in the armor to get the Leaver to stay. These urgent pleas are destined for failure because nothing says, "I'm desperate" like one-sided bargaining. It's the human version of two wolves at a standoff. The beta wolf drops down on his back and exposes his throat to the alpha in return for being allowed to stay in the pack. Big, one-sided concessions, are the hallmark of bargaining in divorce:

"Just tell me what you want."

"Please stay—I'll do anything."

"I'll move out if you give it more time."

"You can keep seeing her/him if you stay with me."

"If you stay, I promise I'll never __________ (fill in the blank)."

The subtext tells us what the bargainer stands to win in the deal: "I'll do whatever it takes to keep you," translates to: "I'll do whatever it takes to hold on to you."

Bargaining may clarify and mend some unaddressed concerns, but it doesn't usually fix longstanding problems. Most couples argue about the same things over and over again. In a marital expression of Darwin's survival of the fittest, the problems that endure in a marriage are the ones that have resisted solution. For this reason, bargaining over the conflicts that have withstood the test of time will likely backfire if proposed too early in the separation, before perspectives and behaviors have had a chance to change.

Remember the ocean rescue scene? Your ex is trying to get away from the relationship and bargaining is another attempt to keep them in the ocean. Hindering escape will not increase trust. Worse yet, when things go wrong or times get rough, you become the perfect scapegoat for the Leaver's unhappiness: "If it weren't for you, I'd be happy!"

Bargaining isn't always a bad thing. Mentally healthy people often make adjustments to troublesome behaviors. Listening to your ex's complaints and drawing from a well of healthy, self-improvement energy can strengthen your relationship later on. But when that desire to change springs from clinging attachment and fear, it can seem desperate and, paradoxically, make your abandonment nightmares come true.

Depression

When denial has hit a brick wall and bargaining goes nowhere, depression spreads its dark blanket of hopelessness. This can be a dangerous time because loss can make life seem as if it's not worth living. Guilt, self-blame, and loneliness can lock you into despair, convincing you the pain is never going to get better. Hopelessness is a symptom of depression, just like sneezing when you have a cold; it's real, but it gets better. The signs and symptoms of depression include loss of concentration, inability to feel pleasure, lack of interest in things you once enjoyed, sluggishness, fatigue, and a loss of sex drive.

Some people experience a greater need for sex during a separation. They long to feel loved, and for many, sex feels like love. Add isolation from other loved ones and over time, the sex drive doubles back into a hunger for physical touch—for human contact.

People in the depressed phase of divorce say:

"It's all my fault."

"There's no use—it's hopeless."

"I give up."

"No one will ever love me again."

"I can't live without him/her."

Ask For Help

If you are in a deep pit, call a friend, call a suicide hotline—whatever it takes to get help right away. Suicidality within the depressed stage of grief doesn't last forever, but a decision to suicide can quickly turn permanent. Here are some toll-free numbers to call if you're feeling suicidal.

- U.S. Suicide Hotline: 800-784-2433
- Depression Hotline Support Group: 800-826-3632
- Suicide Prevention Services Crisis Hotline: 800-784-2433

Case Study: Sade's Unexpected Joy

Sade had been married to her husband, John, for thirty years before he decided he had to be honest with her about being homosexual. He asked for a divorce. A year later, Sade was housebound, living on alimony and a paid-off mortgage. For Sade's 60th birthday, her daughter, Marie, decided to create an incentive to get her mom out of the house. She gave Sade a gift card for a pedicure at a local salon. Her mom had never had a pedicure before, and Marie worried that her mother would stuff the card in a drawer and never use it.

When they visited together after her birthday, Sade gave a glowing report about the pedicure: "I loved it! It was wonderful." Sade explained that when the attendant at the salon pulled her feet out of the warm, soapy water and started massaging her skin, it exposed her pain. It was the most she'd cried since the day John left. Apart from a few hugs she'd gotten from her kids and grandkids, the foot massage was the first time she'd been touched in over a year.

Sade had an emotional reaction to that physical contact. The experience let her see her mistake. She'd spent the last year punishing herself, under house arrest, for the divorce. It was as if her sadness over the divorce had mimicked a power outage during a storm. She spent a long time in the cold and dark, blaming herself for not knowing it was coming. Then, there was that moment when the power was back and the lights came on, and she was so grateful to see again. There is a healing power in touch that lights more than the sensory strip of our brains; skin contact electrifies that vital spark that exists between humans in our world.

Anger

Anger in response to a death can be directed at anyone and anything. Anger during a breakup is usually directed at the Leaver, and the rage can expand into a mushroom cloud of attacks and vengeful actions. In the depression phase, people blame themselves for the separation. In the anger phase, they blame others: their ex, the "other" man or woman, the in-laws.

Anger may feel like a black hole, void of love, but it is more like a white hot light composed of all the colors of the feeling spectrum. Recall in our chapter on myths that the opposite of love is not hate but indifference. Divorce anger is a mix of different emotions not the least of which are fear, love, rejection, sadness, abandonment, betrayal, hopelessness, and helplessness. When you feel angry, take a moment to search for the emotions below the fury. There are bubbles of softer feelings trapped below that hard iceberg. Use them to remember you are more than your rage. Post-traumatic growth will be your reward in the face of all that turbulence because introspection brings you back to the source of your power: self-awareness.

Angry lashing out can be a last-ditch effort to exert control over the Leaver when everything else has failed. But for some, particularly those with a short fuse, it's a starting point—a knee-jerk rage response. If you have a history of physical violence, rage may be the emotional crabgrass that has overtaken your marriage. There are many individuals who have had traumatic histories, including childhood victimization and head injuries, who carry the psychological scars and suffer alterations in the way their brains process information. For these people, the brain becomes more receptive to hitting the gas under pressure while complementary circuits for hitting the brakes are overrun (Siever, 2008). They suffer the negative consequences of their fury in lost relationships and work dismissals. Sometimes behavioral strategies fail to fix the problems and medications are used to quell the misfiring brain circuits. The selective serotonin reuptake inhibitors (like fluoxetine, sertraline and paroxetine) and mood stabilizers have been used with some success in the treatment of destructive anger.

The anger phase of divorce grief can be particularly devastating. Like pouring gas on a house that's already burning, divorce anger can turn a volatile situation lethal. Because of its potential for long-term devastation, divorce anger deserves its own case study.

Case Study: Mark Skips Past Anger and Goes Straight to Rage

Mark was referred for therapy after his wife placed a restraining order on him. He described his reaction when his wife came to their house to pick up her things.

"She was with her boyfriend."

He rubbed his forehead as he recalled the incident.

"At first, I told her it was okay if she came by the house to get her things. She said she would wait until I left for work, but I wanted to show her that I had changed… that I was ready to give her the space she needed. I stayed in the background while she packed. I even pretended that I didn't know the guy was her boyfriend. We almost got through the whole thing without a scene. But then her friend picked my son up from his high chair on the way out, and everything went black. I started cursing… I was grabbing for my son and pushing the guy out of my house. I lost it in front of my wife and my little boy. I didn't mean to do it. He started crying. My wife started yelling at me. It was bad… I just lost it. I lost everything. It's all my fault. She's never going to come back to me now."

Can you see how quickly Mark cycled through the stages from acceptance to anger and then depression? He was like a cowboy trying to ride a bucking bronco of grief. He depended on his strength of will to keep him secure in the saddle. But it was too much to ask in this early stage of grieving. He may have seen glimpses of acceptance, but they hadn't lasted long. He was still in a type of bargaining stage, hoping his wife would see how much he'd changed and decide to come back. Mark was able to hold on for the wrangle until his son came into play. Could you have held on for that same wild ride? Sometimes it's best not to toss your hat into the ring until you've had more time to stabilize.

Let's look at Mark's words and observe the different stages of grief he bounced through during that single interaction.

- ☯ Denial and bargaining: "I wanted her to see that I had changed."
- ☯ Anger: "I started cursing… I was grabbing for my son and pushing the guy out of my house."
- ☯ Depression (self-blame and hopelessness): "I lost everything. It's all my fault," and "She's never going to come back to me now."

If you find it hard to control your anger—or worse, if you have thoughts of homicide—consider it the equivalent of suicidal thoughts in a world of permanent bad decisions. Fantasies of killing your ex or their lover require professional help before they end in disaster. There are newspaper accounts every day describing angry spouses who act out their rage on their ex and even their children. I've spoken to many perpetrators after arrest, and unless they're psychotic, they all share one emotion: regret. By that time, it's too late.

You may think your feelings of rage are uncontrollable, but ask yourself, "Have I ever smashed something that was irreplaceable in the heat of anger?" For most domestic violence cases the typical answer is "No." A rational person, even in the heat of rage, can control their anger enough to avoid throwing their laptop or cell phone against the wall. You can increase the chances of getting what you want if you make an effort to cool the fire with help from someone who can see the big picture. Don't try to deal with these feelings alone if they are boiling out of control.

Acceptance

Most people think the acceptance phase of grief means no longer having intense feelings about the loss. That's not true. Acceptance grows like a tree. It starts as a sapling, but with time and nurturing it grows into a sturdy oak of self-assurance.

One year after his divorce, Ron, a Wal-Mart cashier, walked into our divorce group with a smile. When his turn to talk came around he couldn't hold back.

"Today, I realized that I've accepted my divorce." He leaned forward , "I was listening to the radio, and the song *I Hope You Dance* came on. It's a song about wishing good things for someone you love. It says, 'And when you get the chance to sit it out or dance, I hope you dance.' I realized at that moment that I was singing the words to Chris" (his ex). He sat back in his chair and let out a long exhale. "My heart felt free. I was wishing him happiness, and I was singing the song for myself too. It felt so awesome!"

It had taken Ron a year to reach that state of acceptance. At first, he hoped Chris would die, not dance. He was working his way up the spiral staircase, ascending through denial, bargaining, anger, and sadness with glimpses of acceptance at the top of the stairs. When he sang that song of hope and felt his heart soar, he knew he'd reached acceptance—the kind that didn't bounce around the other phases of grief.

Ron's ability to rediscover his capacity for happiness is a reward of the acceptance phase. His heart was full enough to spill over with good wishes for himself and his ex though they were no longer married.

Don't stop taking the next step on that revolving grief staircase. Ron still cried when his ex wasn't there to see his college graduation a week later. He still took pleasure reading the letter declaring his ex was finally off his health insurance. Acceptance won't lift you up and drop you off in Nirvana for the rest of your life. You'll still have all the natural reactions to the things that tug or snip at your heartstrings. But if you go in with the knowledge that we all repeat the phases, they won't sneak up and take you down. The closer you are to a soul-satisfying acceptance, the better you'll get at recognizing the shift when you slide on a slippery step up the spiral staircase.

The Dreaded Rebound

Before we move on from acceptance, there's a neon sign that blinks the word "Acceptance" under cover of night. It draws you closer offering a false feeling of security while bathing you in its warm glow. It's acceptance's evil changeling, the dreaded "rebound." This isn't tripping on a single step of the spiral staircase as much as tumbling down the center and slamming onto the concrete below. Chuck, a park ranger explained it best: "I started dating to make my wife jealous… now I'm going through my second divorce."

Lots of us take a shortcut past grief by plunging into the soothing waters of a new relationship. I like to call this type of false acceptance "Divorce Imprinting," based on a fascinating phenomenon documented by a Nobel Prize-winning zoologist, Konrad Lorenz. Imprinting is a great explanation for why so many of us fall victim to the rebound. Lorenz discovered the power of imprinting while studying newborn ducklings during their first critical hours after hatching. He noticed that the hatchlings, if caught in time, bonded to anything that moved. They would follow the moving object in the same way they would tag along behind their mother. Imagine the feeling Lorenz must have had when those fuzzy little ducklings started following him wherever he went! It was a fascinating experiment because he also learned that if he waited past those first few critical hours, they would mature past seeing him as Mama and no longer follow when he led. Lorenz' research led to our current understanding of the concept of "critical periods."

Of course, humans are far more complicated and less controlled by instincts than hatchlings, but there is a critical period during loss that makes us vulnerable to the rebound. The need to feel loved, especially early in the divorce when the floor drops out from under us, acts like a critical period. This human version of imprinting cranks up our risk for making unhealthy attachments with the wrong person, simply because they show up at the right time. If we can remember that we are vulnerable during this critical period, we can use it to break free of its dominant force in the early stages of grief. My theory may sound absurd, but many divorce recovery experts caution individuals to avoid making significant changes in their lives or starting serious relationships during the first year of divorce. The rebound effect is most likely to happen during that first critical year, so it's important to be wary in the early months of divorce despair.

During the separation from your ex, it may feel as though you are in a limbo between marriage and divorce, between being in a committed relationship and being free to move on. It is natural to ache for the human contact you had with your partner. Humans thrive on the comfort of physical contact. It releases oxytocin, a chemical known as the "cuddle hormone" because it is also released by mothers caring for their newborns. Touch can be soothing. Being wrapped in the warm embrace of a lover fills a basic physical and emotional need. We associate physical contact with the currency of romantic love, but physical touch can take many forms. Take the case of Sade, the 60-old divorcée who experienced a profound reward from simple massage.

How do you know if you've fallen into a rebound relationship?

1) A rebound typically happens during the critical period after your breakup when you are emotionally distraught or feeling unlovable. During this time, the instinctual need for close contact clouds your capacity to make smart decisions about a new partner.

2) The attraction is based more on a physical and emotional need than on true compatibility with the new person.

3) Fear can play a big part in divorce imprinting—fear of being alone, fear of being unlovable, or fear of being penniless.

4) Anger can be a catalyst for starting a "revenge rebound," which can be especially corrosive to your growth.

5) In a rebound relationship, your new partner takes away your sadness, loneliness, and feelings of failure and unattractiveness through a flood of feel good hormones like dopamine and oxytocin. These cuddle and love hormones act as elixirs for grief and keep you coming back for more.

We are more evolved than new hatchlings, but we have powerful responses to things that make us feel good. Turning to a new partner while in the throes of divorce is the equivalent of turning to cocaine—it's an addictive high. It feels good in the moment, but chances are that in the end, it will leave you depleted and worse off than before you started.

A good rule of thumb that we've learned from teaching divorce classes is that it takes one year of recovery for every four years of marriage. Does that mean that if you're coming out of a sixteen-year marriage, you have to wait four years to have another relationship? No. The formula was developed to help you realize that it takes longer to recover than you think, and the longer you've been married, the longer the recovery time. Rebound relationships not only slow your recovery, but they can also have disastrous consequences.

Case Study: Haley's Rebound

When Haley's husband left her, she felt completely unwanted. Every morning, she'd look in the mirror and stare at her forty-eight-year-old face, searching for wrinkles to prove that no one would ever want her again. She was an investment analyst, and the first thing she said when the topic of loss came up in therapy was, "I'm a worthless commodity in the sexual marketplace."

She was attractive, but it didn't matter because she couldn't see it. All she could see was how her husband had rejected her for a younger woman. Haley was an easy mark for a coworker she'd used as a sounding board for her divorce chronicles. Within a very short time, they were sneaking off on sexual escapades during lunch hour. She avoided discussing it in therapy until the day she came in and announced that she was in love and no longer needed treatment.

Haley's world had grown brighter. She felt alive with an intoxicating happiness. All the grief about her divorce had vanished. She decided that the divorce was the best thing for her after all. She hadn't felt this kind of passion with her husband for years. The sex was "phenomenal" and she wanted to spend every waking minute with this man.

Haley stopped trying to convince her husband to take her back. Not surprisingly, it piqued his curiosity. He found excuses to visit her, but she had no time for him. When he finally confronted her, she explained that she was in love and that she wanted to get the divorce over as quickly as possible. She didn't care that her husband was having doubts about ending their marriage. He even offered to move back into their home, but she would have none of it. Her life had changed for the better, and there was no going back.

Haley got her speedy divorce and married Mike six months later. A week after returning from her honeymoon, the abuse started. Mike had never told her about his problem with anger. While they were dating, there was nothing to be angry about. They were two people who couldn't get enough of each other. With each of them living in their own places and working full-time jobs in separate offices, the opportunities to spend time together were short and passionate. Once they were married, they had loads of time together. The sex was no longer super-charged, but the anger was.

When Mike began yelling and throwing pots at her one night, it was as if a curtain had lifted. She came back to treatment in a panic: "What have I done?" She realized she'd fallen victim to a rebound. For months she beat herself up mentally, while Mike beat her up physically. She couldn't stand the thought of another divorce and bounced in and out of treatment wrestling with shame. She called her ex-husband after a particularly violent episode and told him about the abuse, but he had no pity for her. He said, "I was ready to give up everything for you, but you told me it was over and I should deal with it. Now you deal with this." He hung up before she could say another word. She realized then she had made a mistake; there was no turning back to her ex-husband for rescue.

Haley had rebounded into a new relationship out of fear of being alone and the false intimacy she'd felt with her coworker. She had not taken the time to recover from her grief. She now had two losses to contend with and felt even worse this time.

Water Seeks Its Own Level

Having witnessed several variations on the theme of seeking solace too quickly in a new relationship, we've formulated a theory about why rebounds are doomed to failure. It's the "Water Seeks Its Own Level" theory of relationships. We tend to get involved with people who are at our own level of emotional health.

Consider this: when you're in the middle of an unwanted divorce, you're at a low point, perhaps the lowest point of your emotional life. There is grief to contend with alongside worthlessness, helplessness, and hopelessness. In an effort to fill the emptiness, you may seek out a new partner. But there's a problem: that new lover is falling for you at one of the lowest points in your life! What does that say about the person you're falling in love with? Maybe it means they're at a low point as well. Maybe they have a streak of Florence Nightingale, or it could be this is as high as it gets for them. If you give yourself time to grow—to become that self-sufficient person you've always known you can be, then you'll attract someone who is at an equal emotional place. Taking the time to get back in control reduces the chances of making mistakes that can affect far more than your love life.

Exercise: Journaling

Let's start an exercise that will payoff for a lifetime. If you're not already writing, start a daily practice of journaling. You may not feel compelled to write out your daily thoughts, feelings, or actions, but it's a sure thing you'll be glad you did. You don't have to get fancy. Even plain printer paper will do, as long as you keep track of the date at the top of each entry. Here are at least nine ways that journaling can help you get through the pain of divorce:

1. Journaling captures mental snapshots to help you see how you are progressing. Many people start by writing about the pain. Later, when they reread their early entries, it's as if they were written by someone else: "Was I really that hurt/angry?"

2. Journaling shows you if you're stuck in the same place month after month. If so, it

might be a good time to try a new strategy, perhaps therapy or a support group.

3. Before bedtime, journaling can give your ideas and feelings a place to rest so you can get some sleep.

4. Instead of hurting your ex, you can write about how much you want to hurt him or her, but always make sure to dig deeper and find the emotions driving the anger. This results in far fewer injuries.

5. Journaling is a place to write your goals so you can get back on track when you lose your way.

6. Journaling helps you remember things you've said to your ex and things your ex has said to you, so you don't have to rely on your grieving memory.

7. You can use your journal to pray or to describe ways you see God or a Higher Power working in your life. Looking beyond your marriage to see beauty (it's still out there) can be a great way to counteract feelings of abandonment.

8. A journal can reveal how much your perspective changes from one day to the next.

9. You can give yourself advice in your journal. But don't be surprised when you don't follow it—like when you write "Don't call him… no matter what, don't call." And you call that same night!

Start a Journal Today

At first, you may struggle with what to write, but if you commit to at least 5 minutes with your journal each day, letting that uncertainty sit in your lap, like an abandoned kitty trembling from the cold, something will change. Ideas and thoughts will start flowing and you'll notice your hand flying to keep up with the flood of emotions spilling onto the page. You can journal for longer than five minutes, but this exercise requires that you commit to a meeting with a blank page of your journal for no less than five minutes per day. You don't need to conclude a thought, write in complete sentences, use punctuation, or even try to make sense. The only thing you have to do is pick a time during the day when you have the least distractions, and start writing your way up the spiral staircase.

Chapter Seven Lessons:

- ☯ Grief does not follow a linear path, it is more of a spiral staircase
- ☯ Skipping past the pain of grief creates more losses
- ☯ Building your confidence and self-worth attracts partners who can stand at your level

Part II:

Chapter 8. The Seven Day ACTion Plan

You're at a critical point in your post-traumatic growth. What you do now is going to impact how the rest of the pieces fall into place. For the next seven days, this book will guide you in developing greater psychological flexibility so you can open up to the changes in your life and make them work for you. Our seven-day plan won't make the break up "all better" in a week. But it will teach you the core exercises you need to move past suffering. Just like any skill, whether it's learning to play the piano or working your way toward a black belt, the rewards will surpass your efforts if you practice regularly.

During this next week, you'll be learning principles of Acceptance and Commitment Therapy (ACT). Each exercise will be attached to a core principle that you'll learn first. Most of the exercises are to be done on a daily basis and then repeated. Think of them as different types of workout exercises; like aerobics, yoga, Pilates, weight training, etc. We may teach a specific exercise on a specific day (e.g., separating pain from suffering on Day One), but once you've completed the first seven days, you can do any exercise on any day. The more you work out and practice, the better. With that said, make sure to start the plan by practicing one principle per day. For example, don't skip to Day 2 practices on Day One. At least not for this first week while you're still learning how things work. We want you to get familiar with a specific strategy before moving on to the next. After the first seven days, it will be up to you to pick and choose your practice(s) for each day.

Day One: Suffering is Optional

"To grow is the sole purpose of existence on this planet Earth. You will not grow if you sit in a beautiful flower garden, but you will grow if you are sick, if you are in pain, if you experience losses, and if you do not put your head in the sand, but take the pain as a gift to you with a very, very specific purpose."- Dr. Elisabeth Kübler-Ross

The words you say inside your head can be the greatest barrier to truth. As humans, we use mental dialog to think and plan, but there's a downside, we "fuse" with our thoughts so they seem real, even when they're false. Rather than testing our notions like scientists, we fall victim to the thousands of impressions that zip through our minds each hour of every waking day. Random thoughts are unconsciously elevated from ideas to fact, the way a hundred dollar bill feels more real to Americans than a hundred euros.

If Albert Einstein met anthropologist Margaret Mead and she told him, "I'm so boring," he'd likely be shocked but more importantly, he wouldn't accept her words as truth. Einstein, the wise physicist, would use the scientific method to define "boring." He would study her behavior assuming the null hypothesis: Mead is no more boring than any other human being. He'd observe Margaret in different settings and rate her level of "boringness." How long does she speak and how long does she listen while in conversation? Is her voice animated or dull? Does she behave the same way with friends and family, as she does with strangers? For instance, she may not be very stimulating at a party with new faces but spark great buzz when talking to her best friend about Samoa. If Einstein observed all these variables, he might conclude that Margaret Mead exhibits boring behaviors in some settings but not in others. Because her complaint carries no power over him, he is free to test the boringness while Margaret just accepts it as real, no testing necessary.

We believe the same kinds of untested thoughts during divorce when we tell ourselves, "I'm unlovable." It's easy to fuse with a thought about being unlovable when you focus on the past, like the time your ex said, "I don't love you." But people and events are dynamic. They change in real time. A snapshot of one event doesn't capture the whole picture or the things that will happen a second after the picture was taken. Can you stop yourself from having the thought "I'm unlovable"? No. Thoughts surface in our minds before we can stop them, just ask anyone who's experienced an earworm after listening to a jingle on a TV commercial. Instead of trying to stop the unstoppable, we can take control over the way we interact with the words.

For example, in response to the thought "I am unlovable," you could *refuse to fuse* by detaching in the following ways:

- ☯ Test the thought like Einstein
- ☯ Repeat the thought until the words lose their power
- ☯ Label the thought as a "mind fart" or "mind sweat," to reveal it as a byproduct of mental activity
- ☯ Turn the words into an animal or a color that represents what your mind is doing
- ☯ Inspect the feelings or memories that precede the thought
- ☯ Align with your mind, instead of the thought, by thanking your mind for working so hard trying to understand the world

By now, you can see that refusing to fuse is any action you take to create distance from the words you say in your head. With that distance, a thought can be examined dispassionately and released if it fails to add value. It's like panning for gold. The mind is capable of thinking up great ideas, solving weighty problems like formulas for rockets that take us to the moon. These golden nuggets of the mind get mixed in with dirt and grit, like thoughts about inadequacy and inferiority. You can keep the gold and toss the waste by taking the time to sift through the words your mind produces.

We all walk around on autopilot comparing what's happening and what's supposed to be happening. We think we know what we're seeing, but every single one of our observations is colored by the lens of our perception. Think of how you might respond to seeing your ex at lunch in a nice restaurant with someone who is very attractive: "That cheater!" The alarming thought rises naturally because you have a history with your ex. Let's say they cheated on you in the past. Your perception is also shaped by your expectations of how people are supposed to behave in a marriage, which is to be faithful. The history and expectations create a filter for what you see. Not convinced?

Ask yourself how a stranger might perceive the same scene? They might see two people wearing business suits at a nice restaurant having lunch. Maybe they move in closer to have a listen… "those slides for your presentation are a real winner," says your ex. In this case, the stranger concludes, "Business lunch." and moves on. We're all limited by our filters.

If we stay locked in our perceptions, we can lose valuable information. The truth gets blocked by the things we think we see. We stop challenging ourselves, sinking deeper into a quicksand of assumptions. ACT principles will guide you to see the world as it is. When we bathe ourselves in the crystal waters of reality, it washes away the impurities of social indoctrination. Over this next week, you'll be given the opportunity to wash up and take a look at your relationship through eyes unsullied by untested beliefs.

Pain versus Suffering

Haruki Murakami, a popular Japanese author, said, "Pain is inevitable. Suffering is optional." Before you write off Murakami for victim-blaming people who suffer, let's take a close look at how pain and suffering are different.

Pain is a normal response to injury and it can be either physical or psychological. You feel pain when you cut your finger, bump your head, or break your leg. You also feel pain when a loved one dies, a child goes off to college, or you witness a car accident. Cutting your finger is nowhere near as painful as breaking your leg. Watching your child go off to college is nowhere near as painful as losing your child to cancer. No matter the cause or the intensity, pain lives in the present, and since it's pain… well… it hurts.

Suffering is the non-acceptance of pain, be it loss or some other unwelcomed change. Suffering insists that things be different from the way they are now. Suffering refuses to accept the present because it is too busy reliving the past and fearing the future.

"When suffering knocks at your door and you say there is no seat for him, he tells you not to worry because he has brought his own stool." - Chinua Achebe

The difference between pain and suffering is like the difference between fear and anxiety. Fear is a response to a real and present danger; anxiety is a response to a possible, future threat. Fear is going down the highway and hitting a patch of black ice that spins your car into oncoming traffic. Anxiety is getting in your car and worrying about crashing before you've started the engine. Pain is a response to a real event. Suffering is nursing the belief that the event should never have happened in the first place.

Pain	**Suffering**
Present	Past/Future
Limited	Never-ending
Real	Perceived
Accepts what is	Avoids what is

Have you ever noticed yourself thinking that your ex should still be home where they belong? That they should never have cheated or walked away? They knew the rules and broke them! Things wouldn't be this way if your ex had done what they were supposed to do and fulfilled their vows: "For better or for worse." You can spend your time fantasizing about what should and shouldn't have happened, but it neglects one very important truth: It did happen.

Here is a simple equation that uses principles of Dialectical Behavior Therapy (Linehan, 1993) to illustrate why suffering is a choice:

Pain + Non-Acceptance = Suffering

Suffering requires two things: pain and non-acceptance. Non-acceptance of what? Non-acceptance of the pain. Here is a great example from a therapy session with an Army Ranger who was diagnosed with post-traumatic stress disorder (PTSD) and who suffered daily.

Soldier: My buddy is dead. I watched the bullet go straight through his face as soon as he poked his head out of the turret [of his armored vehicle]. I can't eat. I can't sleep. I don't know what it's like to feel happy anymore.

Elaine: What kinds of things do you think about when you remember him?

Soldier: I think about what a great guy he was. How it should've never happened. We had just rotated shifts. If it had happened five minutes before, it would've been me taking that bullet. I should've been the one manning the turret. It's my fault he's dead.

The pain this soldier is feeling is clear: "My buddy is dead." This is unadulterated pain that comes from the loss of a close friend. His friend is gone, and he will never see him again. You don't have to add anything. It is sad and painful all by itself.

So, what is the non-acceptance?

I asked the soldier to think about what could have or should have happened differently in order to understand the thoughts he had fused with to create his suffering. They could be distilled down to three beliefs:

1) The death should never have happened.
2) The death should have been me, not him.
3) The death is my fault; I could have stopped it.

His refusal to accept the way his buddy died was preventing him from dealing with the pain of his buddy dying. The truth is, his friend is dead and that death cannot be undone. Until he can admit that he's sad because his friend is dead and allow himself to feel the pain of that death, he will continue to suffer. The self-punishing thoughts about how it should have been him instead of his buddy will keep him digging in far-off places instead of finding a resting place for his buddy right inside his own heart. Hindsight is always twenty-twenty. If he knew what was going to happen ahead of time, neither of them would have stuck their heads out of the turret. The time this Ranger spends stoking his non-accepting guilt steals from the time he could devote to his real pain… his grief. Now let's look at an example of someone suffering from a divorce.

Case Study: John Tells Mary He Wants a Divorce

Mary was sitting in the kitchen drinking coffee when John told her he wanted a divorce. Mary loves John and can't stand the pain of him leaving. She wracks her brain thinking about how this can't be happening. She can't accept this separation… she just won't have it!

Mary is consumed with sadness, anger, and sometimes rage. She can barely get out of bed in the morning and she can't stop telling her friends about how unfair it is. One friend tells her to just "kick him to the curb," and "move on." But she can't; she's using all her energy to avoid the pain of losing him.

Mary's non-acceptance has transformed the pain of losing her best friend into suffering. It's natural, it's instinctual to avoid threatening situations. If you avoid going for a walk alone on the African savanna because you could be attacked by a lion, it makes sense. Avoidance is not so logical when you have to check your door lock a dozen times before going to bed because your house was broken into last year. Obsessively checking door locks isn't the only way we avoid pain. In divorce, you check one more time to see if your ex is still over and done with a new lover. You make one more phone call to ask if it "really" is over. You write letters or compose emails asking what you can do to fix things. The fact is, the more you resist the pain, the more you suffer.

Exercise: A Mudslide of Pain

Here's another way of looking at non-acceptance. Pretend you're living on the side of a hill and there's a heavy rainstorm. It rains all day and through the night. The next morning, you hear a noise, so you open your back door to take a look. As soon as you release the latch, the door pops open and mud starts flowing into your house. It's a mudslide. You put your shoulder to the door and push hard to close it, but the mud is too heavy, there's too much of it. The best you can do is slow its progress. You continue to struggle—you won't give up—but no matter what you do, the mud keeps filling your house.

What are three actions you might take if faced with this scenario:

____

____

____

Do any of your actions accept that the mudslide can't be stopped?

What if you release the door, accepting that the mud is going to flow into your house? If you did that, you would be free to consider other options, like opening the front door to let the mud drain out. Yes, there's still going to be a lot to clean up, but not nearly as much as you will have if you keep resisting, while watching your house fill to capacity.

During your divorce, use your energy for the actions that will give you the greatest return. Accepting the pain of losing your relationship can stop your suffering. We already said that pain hurts. There's no getting around that. But there is a difference between hurting for a limited time and suffering for a long time over thoughts about why it shouldn't have happened.

> *PEARL: The things we tell ourselves we cannot or must not have in our lives create suffering.*

So, what does non-acceptance sound like to the person who has been left behind in a marriage? Here are some words that might sound familiar to you:

"This shouldn't be happening."

"She made a vow to stay 'till death do us part.'"

"A good father wouldn't walk away from his family."

"I should've been kinder, more loving, more understanding."

"I won't let this happen."

"I can't live without her."

"I'd do anything to get him back."

Non-accepting statements do nothing to deal with the real pain of loss. The fact that your ex is not with you hurts. You're missing the person you used to talk to about your lousy day at work, the person who took up the slack when you were short on time. You're free to cry, to pound your fists on a pillow, to yell in a safe place. Your feelings are real. Allow yourself to have them. Don't compound the pain by adding layers of resistance. Your pain is real, but you can't run away from it like a lion in the savannah. Accept your emotions for what they are, a part of you; they are not your enemy to be vanquished. It's the resistance that gives them power.

Exercise: Suffer No More

Let's focus on your suffering: Pain + Non-acceptance = Suffering

We don't want to hide your pain; we want to expose it to the light and examine it like we did back in the autopsy room. First, you'll start by identifying the differences between your pain and your suffering. You'll also practice techniques to help you accept pain and reject suffering.

Here are some examples of painful thoughts that stem from divorce:

- "He's moved out."
- "The other side of the bed is empty."
- "I miss her."
- "My marriage is over."

Here are some examples of thoughts that cause suffering due to non-acceptance of the loss:

- "He's insane."
- "It's happened before, and she's always come back."
- "I should have listened better."
- "I can't stand this anymore."
- "This can't be happening."
- "He should have waited until the kids were out of the house."

Watch the words you're using and check for non-accepting thoughts—words like:

- should have
- could have
- can't
- won't

If you notice that you avoid thinking about your sadness and pain, use it to remind yourself that the pain is already there, all you're doing is acknowledging it. When you stop resisting pain, it transforms and drifts away like a racing pulse once you've stopped running.

Exercise: Separating Pain from Suffering

In the table on the next page, list those thoughts that are causing you distress. Notice the difference between painful thoughts, which are genuine reactions to loss, and suffering thoughts, which are focused on avoiding loss. Based on what you've learned about non-acceptance causing suffering, check whether the thoughts are reflections of pain or suffering.

After today, review them weekly. Reevaluate whether you've labeled your thoughts correctly as pain or suffering, and cross off any that have improved. For each one you cross off, try to add another to the bottom of the list. Remember, recovery is a process, and new feelings can emerge as you grieve. If this exercise is working, the symptoms related to suffering will be crossed off faster than the symptoms related to pain. Over time, the pain will naturally lose its fuel.

Exercise: Is It Pain or Suffering?

	List feelings and thoughts associated with your breakup.	**Pain**	**Suffering**
1	Example: *This should never have happened.*		X
2	Example: *I miss him.*	X	
3	Example: *I need to get him to stay.*		X
4	Example: *My heart aches.*	X	
5			
6			
7			
8			
9			
10			
11			
12			
13			
14			
15			

Let's move deeper into your personal experience with a writing assignment that targets the loss of your relationship. This is a *one-time-only* exercise. We won't ask you to repeat it each week like the Pain versus Suffering exercise.

A few chapters ago you performed an autopsy on your old relationship to uncover the toxins that killed it. Let's take time now to give it a proper burial by writing an obituary and filling in a headstone to show respect for what was lost. In this way we can move past the non-acceptance and take our first steps toward grieving.

Exercise: My Relationship Obituary

Begin your obituary by writing the age of your marriage when it ended. List the specific time and place. Was it at the dinner table when your ex said they wanted a divorce? Was it on a Friday night in the bedroom when they packed their bags and walked out? Try to be creative, use words such as "The marriage passed away after a long struggle with ... " or "Our marriage went to be with the Lord ... " Then write down personal information about your relationship.

- ☯ What did you accomplish together?
- ☯ What were your favorite moments?
- ☯ What were your worst moments?
- ☯ What made the relationship special?

Obituary:

My Marriage Headstone

On your relationship headstone, write down a respectful quote that represents your relationship. This is how you want your marriage to be remembered, by others and by yourself. These are words you might want to be saying to your friends and family after your recovery. Here's an example:

Our Marriage Created Two Wonderful Children.
or
We Knew Love for so Long
or
We Learned From Each Other

Resources: You Are Not Alone

You probably had some strong feelings as you wrote your words. You may have cried, felt like throwing something, or noticed a heaviness in your chest. These are all signs of emotional pain. It's your body's language for communicating that something hurts. Listen to it. Avoid the natural tendency to kill the pain with alcohol, drugs and other damaging addictions. Remember that you're grieving but you're not alone. If you are ready to talk and receive help for your pain from others, consider these options:

https://www.meetup.com/topics/divorcesupport/ (Meetup.com info on local people facing divorce)

http://www.parentswithoutpartners.org (info on divorced and single parents near you)

https://www.divorcecare.org (info on local churches offering divorce group)

http://www.goodtherapy.org/learn-about-therapy/issues/divorce (info on therapists near you who specialize in divorce)

http://www.womansdivorce.com (online support for women during divorce)

https://www.dailystrength.org/group/breakups-divorce (Christian-based, for women)

https://forums.psychcentral.com/divorce-separation/

Day One Lessons:

- ☯ The words you say in your head can be the greatest barriers to the truth
- ☯ Pain + Nonacceptance = Suffering

Day 2. Attachment

"Once you stop clinging and let things be, you'll be free, even of birth and death. You'll transform everything."-Bodhidharma

Within the context of an intimate relationship, an attachment is an enduring emotional bond that develops between two people. The security we feel from our emotional bonds can free us to learn and take chances or it can degrade into bondage. Our society, the media, and religious indoctrination shape our beliefs about the bond of marriage. We refer to our spouse as "my better half." We listen to songs that glorify possession: "You belong to me." Popular artists write lyrics that reinforce the belief: "I can't live without you." We're surrounded by a society that insists our lover is as vital as a heart or lung for survival.

Genesis describes the first relationship between man and woman as primordial, with man responsible for producing the first woman: "When the man was asleep, God removed one of the man's ribs and closed up the flesh where it had been. Then the Lord God formed the rib that he had taken from the man into a woman and brought her to the man. So the man exclaimed, At last! This is bone from my bones and flesh from my flesh. This one will be called Woman, because she was taken from Man. Therefore, a man will leave his father and his mother and cling to his wife, and they will become one flesh." (Genesis 2:22)

Not only does this flip our understanding of how the womb functions, but it tells us that man and woman are so inseparable that clinging is not a flaw, but a duty. Our wedding vows foster the same type of clinging attachment with proscriptions like "till death do us part" and "let no man put asunder."

Our culture locks us into a two dimensional world of expectations, teaching us to believe that the person we call husband or wife belongs to us: "My husband," "My wife." More valuable, but not very different from our other possessions: "My cat," "My dog." Even worse, these flat images of our spouse take on the quality of a painting—static, with no variation to how figures relate to one another. We expect permanence in our marriage. We believe things should stay the same, that our loved one should love us forever. Never cheat. Never leave. Our insistence on permanence is one of the greatest challenges we face as humans because the *rule* of nature is *change*, not stasis. In fact, the word stasis is used in medicine to describe stagnation. When blood circulation or lymph nodes become blocked, it is like water with no outlet. Over time, the fluid stagnates and collects bacteria. We understand how this works with the body, but refuse to explore the concept of stasis in our relationships.

Nature provides the seasons. Seasons change throughout the year. The earth rotates on its axis. Daylight changes to night. Imagine what would happen if the Earth stood still. Our life depends on change. We live in a changing body. We grow hungry only a few hours after our last meal because our body burns energy and requires more fuel. Our red blood cells die and are replaced by new ones every three months. Why, then, would we expect love and people to remain unchanged?

On Day One we described how humans fuse with their thoughts. We also fuse with our attachments and our expectations of them. We expect our children to die after us. We feel guilty if we're not able to keep our parents alive and healthy when they're no longer able to care for themselves. We see ourselves as failures if we don't stay married for a lifetime. Fusing with our expectations and attachments threatens our happiness when reality refuses to conform.

A World Without Clinging Attachments

What if you woke up one day in a world where your ex never belonged to you? What if when you were a child, you were taught that no one belongs to you? Not your kids or your spouse. What if your wedding ceremony was used to reinforce the idea that no one was put on this earth as a "soulmate," only for you? Then reality would align with your thoughts and you'd realize that attachments, although alluring as any painting in a museum, can only show you a part of a greater vision. And if you do choose to stand and stare at that one beautiful painting for a lifetime, know that you are also choosing to give up that time with other works of art like sculptures, ancient artifacts, precious jewels, and minerals.

Before you were born, you breathed amniotic fluid. After birth, you could no longer breathe through water and the umbilical cord, the last tie to your mother, was cut. Inside the womb, there were no choices, but there was peace through absolute attachment. Once you were born, you changed so you could survive outside the womb. Your lungs breathed air. Your eyes started recognizing patterns. Your brain adapted to your environment. Your dependency on Mother continued but on a more limited basis. Eventually, you learned to walk and to put food in your own mouth. Nature created us to be independent, to be free of clinging attachments. Our lives depend on our ability to adapt. Our very first relationship was designed with built-in autonomy.

Does all this mean you can never have a long-term relationship because it represents an attachment? Of course not. Humans and even animals can bond for a lifetime. We're at the top of the food chain, not only in terms of survival, but in our ability to love deeply. That can't be a mistake of nature. With love comes attachment, a feeling of connection, and the desire to hold on to the people and things we value. But once we fuse with the desire to hold on, to the exclusion of psychological flexibility and adaptation, it can blind us to our needs and the needs of our loved ones. Then it's time to ask if our natural bond has devolved from healthy love to clinging attachment. What's the difference between healthy attachment and clinging attachment? Clinging insists:

"I will love you as long as you love me back.

"I will love you as long as you don't leave me.

"I will love you as long as you give me what I need."

Clinging attachment is love with a one-sided focus. Healthy attachment is flexible. Like flying a kite, it involves releasing or pulling back depending on the forces you're facing. Martin Buber, a famous twentieth-century philosopher, described the "I/Thou" relationship as an aspirational alternative to clinging. He believed that if I love you as a "Thou" (a person to be respected, with individual rights and desires), then I don't need to depend on you as a prop for my happiness. I can stand on my own, and I can allow you to stand on your own, independent of me. The I/Thou relationship is the Agape, God-like love we referred to earlier as unconditional, no strings attached.

> *PEARL: My love places my loved one in a position of honor, free to make choices regardless of whether they offer me comfort.*

Your life is unique. It cannot be fully understood by any other person. Orson Welles once said, "We're born alone, we live alone, we die alone. Only through our love and friendship can we create the illusion for the moment that we're not alone." Notice he used the word *illusion* to describe how love acts like a drug to ward off the dread of being solo. Even with a bedmate by your side, when you lay your head down at night, only you can hear your thoughts.

Right now, you've probably read all this and think, "I'll take the blue pill," convinced that staying married will make you happy. But there's a difference between wanting to stay married and *having* to stay married. The "have-to" is the clinging attachment, it keeps you hooked to an outcome. When you're hooked, there's no place to go, no way to walk a few steps to peek around the corner to see the new opportunities within your reach.

Eastern philosophies and Buddhist teachings caution that the desire to possess people and things is at the root of unhappiness. A Chinese proverb reads, "The Great Way is not difficult for those not attached to an outcome. When not attached to love or hate, all is clear and undisguised."

Being attached to your ex and feeling lost without them is not your fault. You've been programmed for years to see marriage through one plane of awareness: "Till death do us part." But, once you see how your clinging attachment is keeping you stuck, the desire for a specific outcome for your marriage will feel more like a ball and chain than a pot of gold.

Pearl: In life, change is the rule, not the exception.

Case Study: Dan's Clinging Attachments

Dan loved Leigh and his two girls. They were his greatest joys, but like the Roman god, Janus, his pleasure had two faces. When things were going well and reality matched his expectations—a beautiful wife, obedient kids with good grades, he felt proud and happy. But when Leigh put on weight after her pregnancies and became moody from hormones, he responded with impatience. "Let me coach you, the exercise will help you lose weight and take off the bitchiness." Once, when he saw his younger daughter fighting with a boy on the school bus, he boarded without permission, ready to fling her attacker off the vehicle. The bus driver grabbed him just in time. The next day, Dan was informed by the principal that his daughter had started the fight. It was as if Dan's clinging attachment magnified normal life problems to the size of a billboard advertising his inadequacy as the man of the family. In his mind, he was their representative, their protector, and if they weren't happy or "acting right", it was his fault.

When Leigh moved out, Dan begged for another chance. He promised to change, he offered to go to church with her and the kids again. When that didn't work, he offered to sleep in a separate room, guaranteeing to keep things platonic.

"I won't touch you. If I do, you can throw me out."

Leigh threw him out anyway, saying, "I need space. I can't have you moping around like Linus without his blanket."

Reluctantly, Dan moved into a one-bedroom apartment. When he thought of Leigh, his heart raced and he felt panicky because she really was his security blanket. Alone, he was just a "working stiff." With Leigh, he was a husband, a father, a protector, and it all gave him value he didn't believe he possessed on his own. Dan didn't know how to cook and he didn't like the crowds when he went food shopping. While he was home with his family, he occasionally played cards with friends but most of the time he came home from work exhausted, preferring to nestle into the couch and watch TV. Leigh, the girls, and his occasional calls to his mother were his miniature support system. Alone in his apartment he felt vulnerable, with no family to protect or to protect him.

Sometimes he had small victories, like the time he made fajitas with the meat rare and juicy. Such a difference from Leigh's charred steaks. But thinking about her cooking made him feel anxious, and that delicious meal became lost in his desire to be back home. Dan's apartment had become a prison cell with a padlock of suffering.

Today is the day to remind yourself that your ex is not your property. You do not own this person, or any other person, no matter what society tells you. You do own your thoughts and feelings. You're alone but you're still a whole person, whether married or single.

Here are two exercises for detaching. They both have to do with changing the belief that your ex is a possession. The first guides you toward releasing the assumption of ownership and the second one illustrates a higher form of love that we referred to earlier as agape, love for all things.

Exercise: No Trespassing

Imagine you've placed a number of signs all over your ex. They all say something about staying off your property. They read:

- ☯ "Keep Off the Grass."
- ☯ "Trespassers Will Be Shot."
- ☯ "Private Property."
- ☯ "Do Not Enter."

Your ex is a black-and-white cartoon with these signs propped up all over their body. One sign is sticking up above their head, another on their chest, one in each hand, one on each leg, and so on. Now say the words: "Property is owned; people are free." Picture yourself pulling out the "Keep Off The Grass" sign from your ex's head. Imagine the cartoon head transforming into your ex's head and their eyes open and look around. You may notice a thought or feeling surface as you remove that sign. No matter what the thought or feeling, label it and acknowledge its presence (anger, resentment, sadness). Then say, "Thank you," to your mind for participating in this exercise.

Once again, say the words "Property is owned; people are free" and remove the next sign from your ex's chest. Imagine their chest transforming from a cartoon to a human, their chest starts expanding and contracting with each breath of air. Now move down to the left arm and remove the sign that reads "Trespassers Will Be Shot." Say the words again: "Property is owned; people are free." The left arm is now real in your mind's eye. Move over to the right arm and remove the sign that reads "Private Property." See how that arm transforms from cartoon to a real human arm. Say the words "Property is owned; people are free," while removing the next sign from your ex's left leg. Notice how the left leg changes from cartoon to human. Repeat the words "Property is owned; people are free," while removing the "Do Not Enter" sign from the right leg. Notice how your ex's right leg changes from cartoon to human. Before ending this exercise, observe your ex's entire body now in its human form, breathing in its natural state with no signs pinned on. Finish the exercise by again repeating the phrase "Property is owned; people are free."

Exercise: Cultivating Agape Love

Imagine you're holding on to a leash that's attached to your ex's neck. Your ex can only go so far before they reach the end of the leash and the collar tightens. You realize: "This isn't a loving relationship," so you decide to remove the leash. In order to do that, you have to figure out what's keeping it in place. Consider the behaviors you're using to keep your ex attached to you:

- ☯ Refusing to listen to their requests for space
- ☯ Withholding or spending money to punish
- ☯ Limiting time with the children to manipulate their feelings
- ☯ Calling or texting frequently
- ☯ Checking to see where your ex is or who they are with

Finish this exercise by writing the following sentence in your journal: "True love does not need a chain to hold it in place."

Day 2 Lessons:

- ☯ Nature created us to grow independent and be free of clinging attachments
- ☯ True Love does not force our beloved to make decisions that support our comfort

Day 3: The First Day of the Rest of Your Life Without Judgement

"Buddhists have always known it, physicists now confirm it. Nothing that happens is an isolated event. The more we label something, the more we isolate it. The wholeness of life becomes fragmented through our thinking."- Eckhart Tolle

Your mind is trying to solve a problem. Let's call the problem: "My spouse is leaving, but I want them to stay." Your brain says, "We've solved problems before. We can solve this one. Just keep thinking. Figure it out!" Problem-solving makes sense to the brain. It's why human beings survived while faster, stronger creatures died off. Our species figured out what we needed to stay alive (tools, fire, shelter) and it worked. In response to divorce, your problem-solving mind is doing some heavy lifting trying to find a solution. Except, in this case, the burden and the solution don't exist in the physical world. You can shoot a charging rhino, but you can't stop a stampede of panic and mourning. With each failing problem-solving strategy, your burden grows heavier with disappointment until your confidence buckles from the weight. All that work to prevent pain is like resisting the mudslide at your back door. The problem is solved not by pushing harder, but by recognizing that resistance is working against you.

You've probably heard people use the phrase "It is what it is." The words have become a mindfulness motto because it acknowledges that something has happened, with no value assigned to the event. Say, for example, that your ex has moved out and you announce, "She moved out," followed by, "It is what it is." The phrase stands alone. It adds no layer of judgment, no fault, no blame for you or them—it's just an acknowledgment that you are no longer living together. When we take the judgment out of a thing, it allows us to clear our mental filters of "rightness" and "wrongness." Once the judging is wiped away, we're free to make decisions based on the things we can control. The goal is not to eliminate pain—it's to accept what life brings without falling victim to its "goodness" or "badness." Then, we are free to embrace Full Catastrophe Living.

The Man Without Judgment

A father and his son owned a horse. The father and son loved one another, and they both loved their horse. They were living a satisfying life together until one day someone stole the horse. Even though he loved the horse, the father did not feel angry. His son asked, "Why aren't you upset about our horse being stolen?" The father said, "It's neither good nor bad. The future is in God's hands." And the father went about the work of plowing his field and leading a purposeful life. A few days later, the horse not only returned but also brought two wild mustangs following close behind. The father and his son were astonished at the bountiful gift. They set about training the mustangs and felt even happier than they had owning just the one horse. But the next day, as the son was riding one of the mustangs, it reared. He fell off and broke his leg. The son said, "I have the worst luck! Don't you feel sorry for me?" The father said, "It's neither good nor bad. The future is in God's hands." And the father went about his work of taking care of his son and horses and leading a purposeful life. One week later, the father and son heard a knock on the door. It was a conscription officer gathering up names for a war draft. The officer took one look at the son's leg and said, "We can't take him; he can't walk, let alone run!" And so, the father and son were able to continue tending their horses and leading a purposeful life in their home together.

This story is a lesson in the problems of judging and predicting. We don't always know whether an event is good or bad. We have no crystal ball to determine the future. The father could have cursed the heavens for taking his horse or allowing his son's leg to break, but he held fast to his understanding that there is no way to predict the future. He also stayed open to a perfection in all things instead of attaching to a specific outcome. He believed there is a divine order to the happenings in life. If you don't like the religious bent to the perfection in God's plans, this is a good time to examine your philosophy about why things happen in life. You can believe in a perfect order to Full Catastrophe Living without forcing yourself to have faith in an Almighty power that guides each event. It is also possible to believe in a random universe where nothing is perfect and still embrace the unpredictability of life.

Case Study: Dan Surrenders Judgment

A few weeks into his therapy, Dan was in a panic. He'd left the vault open at work, and some sensitive documents were missing. We talked about it in session:

Dan: My commander told me to meet him and my first sergeant in his office after this. I'm in trouble… probably getting an Article 15. First my marriage and now my career.

Elaine: It sounds like you're fusing with thoughts about the worst thing that could happen.

Dan: Could happen? Leigh is gone. I'm living in a freakin' shoebox, and now I'm in trouble at work. This stuff is all happening now, in real time. How am I overreacting?"

Elaine: I didn't say overreacting, I said fusing with your thoughts. You said, "first my marriage and now my career," as if you could predict what your commander is going to do.

Dan: I'm not thinking straight.

Elaine: What can you tell your commander?

Dan: I can tell him I'm having a hard time with my wife wanting a divorce. That I haven't been sleeping and my game is off.

Elaine: That's all true. You made a mistake and you're owning up to that. Keep the focus on what's happening now.

Dan: But what if I lose my job? I'll be homeless!

Elaine: You can listen to the judgments your mind is coming up with and respond by saying, "Thank you for worrying about me, mind, but there's no way of knowing how this is going to turn out. In the meantime, I'm going to be honest with my commander about how much I love my job and come up with things I can do to keep this from happening again."

Dan: That makes sense 'cos I can't stop judging, and I do suck at predicting. Like when Liz was born and I thought she'd die from apnea. She made it through, and there's nothing wrong with her. And the time I thought my mother was going to be fine after surgery, but she ended up in hospice and died two days after I left. She seemed fine.

Elaine: It's not just you Dan, we all want to believe we can predict what's going to happen. But time and experience teach us to wait and see because most of the time we expect things that never happen and we don't expect things that do happen. Staying open is how we learn patience.

Dan: It's like they say, "The more I know, the more I realize how much I don't know."

Elaine: And, that's called wisdom.

The next time I talked to Dan he explained that his commander punished the lapse with a Letter of Admonishment, the military version of a slap on the hand. Dan's commander told him he respected Dan's history of hard work. The First Sergeant, a type of workplace foreman, had already told the commander that Dan was in distress over his break up before the open-vault incident. Checks had already been put in place, which is how they discovered the problem in the first place. Dan had garnered respect at his work center, and although his negligence was like a withdrawal from his work account, he'd banked so many hours of dedicated service, the incident had little impact on his reputation or his career.

There's a popular phrase that goes, "The only way to get past the pain is to go through it." When you take the judgment out of pain, it's like going through hell with a fire hose. The pain is still there, but it doesn't consume you. You can grow from adversity by confronting your judgmental thoughts. Think back to the story of *The Man Without Judgment.* You have no idea how your divorce or separation is going to play out in your life. Ironically, Dan's anxiety had attached itself to an outcome, not a hopeful, "this is all going to work out" outcome, but a scary shadowy outcome of losing his job.

Some people believe that nothing in life happens randomly and that everything happens for a reason. No matter what you believe, we know from research on post-traumatic growth that the greater the challenge, the greater the potential for growth.

Exercise: My Life Without Judgment

Instead of asking, "Why did this happen to me?" take the role of the man without judgment. Make a list of things that have happened in your life that you expected to turn out negative but turned out positive.

____

____

____

Exercise: My Judgments

Write down three judgments you made today. It could be about your appearance, your performance at work, your separation—anything that you labeled as "good/bad", "great/terrible", "beautiful/ugly."

Example: *He's never coming back.*

____

____

____

Exercise: Bursting Your Bubbles

Like your thoughts, it is not possible to stop judgements from rising like mind bubbles, but it is possible to pop them. Using the three judgments from your day (above), write down how you could go back and reframe your judgments. Use this poem by Alberto Caeiro to guide your thoughts:

"If I knew I was going to die tomorrow,
And Spring came the day after tomorrow,
I would die peacefully, because it came the day after tomorrow.
If that's its time, when else should it come?
I like it that everything is real and everything is right;
And I like that it would be like this even if I didn't like it.

Reframe Example: *He may or may not come back, I have no way of knowing. Either way I'm going to keep moving forward.*

____

____

____

Day 3 Lessons:

- ☯ We don't always know whether an event is good or bad because we cannot predict the future
- ☯ Attaching to a specific outcome narrows our vision and our options

Day 4: Radical Acceptance

"It is believed that in the midst of a fight, a bull can find his own particular area of safety in the arena. There he can reclaim his strength and power. This place and inner state are called his querencia. As long as the bull remains enraged and reactive, the matador is in charge. Yet when he finds his querencia, he gathers his strength and loses his fear. From the matador's perspective, at this point the bull is truly dangerous, for he has tapped into his power."—Tara Brach

You've learned how suffering is the by-product of non-acceptance. The lesson can sound fatalistic, suggesting that surrendering to pain is the key to well-being. But today's topic on Radical Acceptance is going to unlock a discovery about the importance of action. Today is all about grabbing the stick shift, letting out the clutch, and hitting the gas, leaving non-acceptance far behind.

Our American culture teaches us that acceptance is for losers. We learn not to accept any outcome unless it suits us. If life gives you lemons, well then, make lemonade! We're a successful society, so there must be some advantage to this never-give-up mentality. Indeed, we can achieve great things when we set our minds on an objective, pushing past any obstacle that stands in our way.

But what happens when we set our sights on an outcome we can't control?

Groucho Marx once said, "I intend to live forever or die trying." The quote is a humorous way of saying there are limits to our influence.

Radical acceptance is a concept within ACT that allows us to push past the noise to reach the signal. It is a mindset for dealing with reality as it is, right now, in this moment—without bending it to our will or running from it. Don't mistake the word acceptance for passivity. It's not like saying, "Oh well, I have no power over my life, so I guess I have to give up." Unlike helplessness, radical acceptance is an active and deliberate way to take control, the way zig-zagging up a steep mountain lets you breathe, take in the scenery and make it to the top without a heart attack. You can think of it as "radical truth" because it pushes past how we wish things could be in order to negotiate reality. This allows us to create attainable goals Jerry's story will explain how Radical Acceptance works.

Case Study: Jerry's Surprise

Jerry had been married to Mika for three years. The couple married after eight years of living together because Mika wanted to have children. After months of not using birth control, the couple had no success. Jerry noticed that Mika was becoming more irritable and their sex life was turning play into work. Mika would want Jerry sexually when she was ovulating but wasn't interested in lovemaking the rest of the time.

"The passion was gone," Jerry said. "I felt like a dog performing for my master."

Jerry stuck with it, though. He loved Mika and wanted to make her happy. After three years of trying, Mika told Jerry she didn't want to be married anymore.

He couldn't believe it.

"I said, 'You've got to be kidding me. I've been working all this time to give you what you wanted, and now you're dumping me?'"

Jerry was heartbroken. He came to therapy feeling like a failure. He couldn't let go of the idea that all his time with Mika was wasted. He felt angry and abandoned. His pain had turned into suffering. During one particular session we discussed Radical Acceptance.

Jerry: She used me.

Elaine: You feel cheated. What can you do about it?

Jerry: I can't do anything about it because she won't listen to me. Her mind is made up—she's gone.

Elaine: Why don't we try a radical acceptance exercise?

Jerry: I'll try anything. This whole thing is driving me crazy.

Elaine: Okay. What do you want to see happen?

Jerry: I want us to get back together and be happy.

Elaine: What part of that desire is under your control.

Jerry: None of it. I told her I wanted her to come back home, but she won't listen to me.

Elaine: You still have control over something.

Jerry: Like what?

Elaine: Were you ever happy before you met Mika?

Jerry: Well, sure I was. In fact, I used to have a lot of fun with my friends before I met her. We'd go four-wheeling and scuba diving… but that was a long time ago.

Elaine: You say you were happy before you met Mika. Can you control Mika … her happiness, her actions?

Jerry: Nope. God knows I tried.

Elaine: Can you control what you do about her decision to leave?

Jerry: Yeah, I guess so, but I get so pissed off. I can't think straight and then I just lose it.

Elaine: When someone hurts us, we react. Normally, it's some kind of anger. We turn that anger in, toward ourselves, or out, toward the person whose hurting us. Either way, the pain is real and needs to be respected.

Jerry: Yeah, but I'm letting my emotions take over completely. They just flare up before I can get them under control.

Elaine: You can't control whether an angry or betrayed feeling is going to rise to the surface. That's "symptom control." It doesn't work. But you can control how you react to the feelings when you notice they are there. How do you think you could do that?

Jerry: Well, I have control over how much I curse over it.

Elaine: Okay. What else?

Jerry: I have control over calling her. I have control over what I tell myself. Like sometimes I tell myself, "She's a witch—she's not worth it," and then sometimes I say, "Our relationship was really sucking toward the end. She did me a favor!"

Elaine: That's true. You can control how you judge what happened to you. You can control what you say to yourself. And you can control whether you stay home or go out and explore your life. You can even control how you respond to Mika.

Jerry: That's a lot of control. I wish I could believe that.

Elaine: You can have pain and still commit to the other things that matter in your life, like reconnecting with scuba diving buddies or making new friends.

Jerry struggled with his thoughts about Mika. He wanted to get out again, but his ruminations over the divorce kept him stuck at home, watching TV and eating frozen yogurt. To break the cycle, we introduced him to "the pink elephant," a technique based on a thought suppression experiment by Wegner and his colleagues in 1987. The technique is quite useful during those times when you can't get your mind off your ex.

ACT - Pink Elephant Technique

Here are your instructions:
Don't think about a pink elephant.
Start now.
Close your eyes and do not think of a pink elephant for the next 60 seconds.
After the minute is up, read on.

Were you successful or did you still see a pink elephant in your mind's eye? If you were unsuccessful, don't worry. It's normal. When you tell yourself not to think about something, you're already thinking about it. If it's a really important something, like your ex, it's even harder to push the thought out of your consciousness.

This isn't a technique for escaping pain—it's about learning to shift your focus to things that are under your control. In Jerry's case, he needed to think about leaving the house instead of clinging to Mika.

> Here are your new instructions:
> Surrender to the pink elephant.
> Go ahead and think about that fat rosy pachyderm as much as you want.
> Are you doing it? Good.

Now, describe the most beautiful sunset you've ever seen. Do you remember where you were? What the colors looked like? Describe as much of it as you can recall.

____

____

____

What happened to the pink elephant while you were writing about the sunset? Were you still focused on the elephant? For most people, the answer is "No." The reason is that by adding a different thought, you have a new focus. Before, you were trying to stop your thought about a pink elephant. This puts you in a struggle against your mind, which is like a tug of war against yourself. But when you give up the struggle and target a different goal, your mind takes its rightful place as your ally. Think of it as a truce with your anguish. Your reward: the pink elephant stops charging while you gaze at the glow of the setting sun!

The same can happen with thoughts of your ex. When you find yourself obsessing, don't struggle. Make a peace treaty with your mind. Think about something you want in your life that is under your control. For instance, what fun things did you like to do when you were younger, before you were ever involved in a romantic relationship? Was there a hobby, a cause or a sport you loved?

It took several months for Jerry to embrace his pain and to accept Mika's decision. It didn't happen all at once—it never does. But when he radically accepted his loss without trying to change her mind, he began to explore. He decided to create friendships by accepting invitations to socialize again. His friends tried hooking him up with new girlfriends, but he avoided dating during the critical imprinting period. He kept all his relationships platonic for the first year. After that, he started to test the waters. One night, he went out to dinner with a group who met at a grand opening for a local Italian restaurant. One woman stood out from the crowd. Her name was Joan, and she worked as a professor at the local university. They began dating. The two had so many things in common that he couldn't believe she was real.

In therapy, Jerry said, "If I had to list everything I wanted in a woman, I wouldn't have the brainpower to think up all the stuff I see in Joan."

Jerry grasped the concept of radical acceptance. After a couple of failures, he realized it was time to let Mika be Mika without his interference. Radical acceptance gives us a method to accept pain without the judgment. Instead of struggling with the thought, "I can't stand this," Jerry accepted that although it was painful, there was no way of predicting the impact of his divorce. He realized he had the power to stay open and focus on his life purpose. He made a choice not to give up on love. He accepted the pain of his loss and his suffering ended.

ACT teaches us to use radical acceptance like an addict practices the serenity prayer. The challenge is to change the things we can and to accept the things we cannot. Accepting the things you cannot change doesn't mean pretending to like them. Like the father in *The Man Without Judgment,* acceptance refuses to assign a "goodness" or "badness" to events in life because we can never really know how one event will affect another. Once you learn this principle of acceptance, and use it, your life will change.

You've probably heard the joke about the man who loses his keys and looks for them under a streetlight. His friend says, "Why are you looking over there? You dropped your keys over here, next to your car." The friend says, "Because this is where the light is." Radical acceptance is accepting that you can't prevent the night, or go back in time before dropping your keys, but you can use a flashlight to look in the right place.

Radical acceptance does not mean passively accepting everything that happens. It allows you to focus your actions like a laser beam, on the things you can control. When you set a target, it frees you to use your energy more efficiently. So instead of following in Groucho Marx's footsteps, trying to live forever, you can skip the false trail and start living now.

Accepting the Separation Is Taking Control

During your separation, you'll be tempted to reconnect with your ex. But, before you make that visit, dial that number, or send that text, ask yourself, "Am I accepting the truth of our separation or is this a way of avoiding pain?" If you're avoiding pain, then step away from the door or put down the phone because the only contact you'll be making is with your suffering.

Losing your relationship feels like an amputation, pain messages from the loss pulse through your nervous system like a phantom limb. Of course it hurts. But, by denying your ex their right to pull away, you're sending a signal of your own: "I don't accept this pain." This would make sense except the pain is already there and the separation has already happened.

Let's move closer to the truth by building your strength to endure your loss. We'll start by focusing on two behaviors that are *immediately* under your control:

1) Making contact: Recall from our Myths chapter that your ex has left the relationship—not you. You can control your half of the relationship by listening and committing to right action.
   a) If your ex says, "Don't call me." Listen. Adjust to the request. Don't call. Otherwise, your behavior says, "You're mine and I don't have to respect your boundaries."
   b) If your ex makes contact as if you're still in the old relationship. Listen. Remind yourself, the old relationship is dead. Respond in a way that acknowledges that the old relationship is gone.
   c) If your ex makes contact wanting to get back together. Listen. Remember the lessons of the autopsy room. Decide if this can become a new, healthy relationship. Ask for professional help if you need guidance.
2) Self-Care: Reading this book and working on the exercises is a way of taking control.
   a) Your ex can tell you, "Stay away." But you get to decide what to do with your life while you're apart, like exercising for stress relief, going out, making new friends, or reading books. No one can tell you how to love yourself. Well they can try, but you get to decide what's right for you.

b) Perhaps you're afraid that accepting the end of your relationship means you will never be happy again or that you will never be able to recover. Notice whether you are fusing with a fear of inadequacy: "I'm too old… too fat… too dull… too unlovable." The specifics don't matter—the fear is that there is something wrong with you, that there is something missing that only your partner can provide.

Consider Henry Ford's quote: "If you always do what you always did, you'll always get what you always got." You're taking control by making a conscious decision to accept the change of your separation. After all, you do have a choice: accept it or fight it. When you make the choice to accept it, you're also giving yourself a present— the gift of a new relationship with yourself and your ex.

Here are some questions to help you determine if you're accepting the separation:

- ☯ Do you drop by your ex's house or work unannounced?
- ☯ Do you call whenever the impulse strikes?
- ☯ Do you ask whether your ex is seeing anyone?
- ☯ Do you offer to do things for your ex (fix the toaster, do the laundry, pick up the mail)?
- ☯ Do you track your ex's whereabouts?

If you answer yes to any of these, then you are not accepting the reality of your new life. Here's one technique to help you accept the separation. Go to the Contacts information on your phone and change your ex's name to:

- ☯ "Reply later"
- ☯ "Detach"
- ☯ "Do not call"
- ☯ "No suffering"
- ☯ ____________________ (use your imagination and add your own)

Using a label that reminds you to do something different when you want to call, keeps your behavior in line with your goals. If they call you, consider the option of letting it go to voicemail. This gives you time to think instead of reacting in the same old way. By taking these actions, you're signaling an increased ability to take care of yourself and acceptance of the separation. You're respecting a new boundary with your ex and giving yourself permission to take your time to grow.

Exercise: Things I Still Control

So what are the things you can control? Read through the following and check the items that are important to you, then add some of your own.

- ☐ Taking care of myself during the separation
- ☐ Remembering not to judge events
- ☐ Designing my own purposeful life
- ☐ Deciding what's important to me (setting priorities)
- ☐ Asking for help from friends/family
- ☐ Joining a support group

Add your own below:

____

____

____

What control do you have over your physical health?

____

What control do you have over your mental health?

____

What control do you have over your social life?

____

What control do you have over your spiritual life?

____

Exercise: I Believe in Love

A person who believes in love will find it everywhere because love floats around us like radio-waves. Have you ever gone on a long trip in your car with your radio set to an open frequency? Eventually, that frequency will pick up a radio station, and you'll hear something—some music or an announcer. This happens because your channel remains open while moving in your chosen direction.

Picture your ex in your mind and say, "I believe in love." List places where you can find love apart from your ex. Doing this exercise will help you grow in your understanding that you are a whole person, capable of sharing love regardless of any loss or changes you encounter. Happiness happens when you drop the chains of clinging attachment and allow your spirit to travel unharnessed.

Example: *I can find love volunteering at a homeless shelter.*

Example: *I can find love by connecting with supportive family.*

Example: *I can find love while visiting an old friend living in Italy.*

____

____

____

Day 4 Lessons:

- Radical acceptance is accepting where you are without the filters so that you take control of the things you can change and release your grip on the things you can't
- Accepting the end of your relationship as you knew it is taking control

Day 5: Mindfulness Practice

"Curiosity has its own reason for existence"-Albert Einstein

You've learned about mindfulness practice as a companion to ACT throughout this book. This method is powerful and its applications in psychology have exploded. Maybe it's because the model is so simple. Mindfulness can be defined as moment-to-moment awareness of yourself and your environment without judgment or criticism. After hearing this definition, one anxious patient said, "But if I stop judging, I'll have no thoughts at all!" She's not alone. We all have a natural tendency to categorize things into good-bad, approach-avoidance, love-hate. It's the judgmental thinking we described during Day 4 that assumes we have the power to predict.

The practice of mindfulness cultivates curiosity and compassion as mental guardrails for your classification-loving brain. Although it started with Buddhist meditation, mindfulness has been adopted by Western medicine through the efforts of Jon Kabat-Zinn, who used it in 1979 to help patients at the University of Massachusetts Medical School reduce their stress and pain. The model has gone viral across all kinds of communities and programs, including schools, hospitals, prisons, military, and veteran's programs. With thousands of studies and a proliferation of programs adopting it, this strategy is worth your attention.

Experts in mindfulness use practical techniques for getting us to recognize the short half-life of our emotions. Think about it. How long have you ever held on to a single emotion? The average person experiences a multitude of feelings over the course of a day. Most feelings are repeats, but none stay for long unless they are fed and watered by your thoughts. You may feel sad for much of the day because of grief, but there will still be spaces in time when you forget to feel sad, especially if you work or have other distractions. That's because feelings change from moment to moment. Although our emotions change, we don't notice these shifts consciously. To detect them, you have to practice observing.

If I dropped a water hose on your lawn and half-opened the spigot, you would see water gurgling across your grass— boring. But if I pushed the nozzle into a bright red balloon, well then you would see the water take shape. Practitioners of mindfulness love to use metaphors to help core principles take shape. Metaphors speak to our unconscious mind so that insights keep pulsing below the surface of our awareness long after we've moved on to new ideas or the next page in this book.

Waves of Emotion

Waves are the most common metaphor used in mindfulness training to describe the transience of emotions. Picture your emotions as ocean waves. Some are big, so big that they crash over your head and take you down. Other waves are gentle, going barely unnoticed as they lap at your toes. The important thing is, each wave will come and go. Waves don't get stuck and neither will your emotions if you observe them without judging. You might argue that the emotions surrounding a breakup are more than waves—they are great tsunamis that sweep you up and drop your exhausted carcass on a remote mountain peak. But that would be a judgment and we want to practice staying curious in order to avoid getting "hooked" by a single emotion, no matter how powerful.

Spinning the Emotions Carousel

Consider a more picturesque metaphor that describes not only the ways feelings change but how they are all connected. Imagine you could place your emotions on a carousel and spin the whole platform with one good pull. You would see anger, discovery, fear, wonder, amusement, jealousy, sorrow, fatigue, excitement… all spin by with no single feeling lasting longer than another. You have no special attachment to any one of these emotions because you have made a decision not to judge them. So, they all go by in a big rainbow of mood colors.

Now imagine that you saw sadness go by, but it bothered you.

"I can't have sadness on this lovely carousel. It's too painful to look at. I've got to take it out."

You place your hand on the carousel to stop it. Now what happens? You're face-to-face with sadness and it doesn't feel good. You want to extract it from the carousel, but it won't come off. In fact, the harder you try, the more it gets stuck in place. Now you notice anger on the left. You spin the carousel to grab hold of anger—that one feels just as bad as the sadness, but maybe it will come off if you pull hard enough! As you turn the carousel to grab hold of anger, you go right past wonder and amazement.

"That's okay," you tell yourself. "If I can just get anger and sadness out of there, only the good emotions will be left, and then this will really be a gorgeous carousel."

But here's the problem: You didn't realize that each of the emotions on your carousel is connected to every other one.

If instead, you look at the carousel as a whirlwind ride where the emotions all have their place, all offering a rich array of experiences, then any emotion can pass by without getting you hooked.

Here are some key mindfulness concepts:

- ☯ Feelings change spontaneously if respected but can become stuck when resisted
- ☯ Staying in the moment helps feelings move freely
- ☯ Staying curious without judging creates an opportunity for awareness

Mindfulness teaches us how to be our authentic selves. What does that mean? Let's start by looking at how we change to suit others. From the time we're little, our parents teach us to control our emotions: "Big boys/girls don't cry." Like the story of Adam and Eve hiding their nakedness from God, we're taught to hide and feel ashamed of our vulnerability: "Look at that man over there. He sees you crying. He thinks you're a big baby." Even worse, some parents threaten their kids to get their emotions in check: "Stop with the waterworks, or I'll really give you something to cry about." We eventually grow up, but those messages keep playing in our heads like old rough and tough John Wayne movies. We even feel uncomfortable when we see others crying or shaking in fear. The next time you see a commercial for a pet rescue charity, watch for the big-eyed puppy trembling on camera. It's a proven technique that increases your chance of taking action. We don't like seeing distress. You'd be surprised at how many doctors will pull out their prescription pad and write a prescription for tranquilizers because a patient cries in their office. These "negative" emotions scare professionals just as much as they do the untrained.

When we're afraid of something, we label it "bad" or "pathological." We make it our goal to force that bad thing to go away. If you knock out a bad feeling -- touchdown! You've achieved success! But here's another problem: What happens when that bad feeling comes back? And how much time and energy are you prepared to spend on something that keeps coming back, no matter how hard you try to ditch it? Some people will spend a lifetime chasing after that pain-free carrot dangling over their heads. Worse yet, they cut off an important part of themselves because they buy into the social brainwashing that insists: "This isn't how I'm supposed to feel."

What's the alternative? Mindfulness teaches us a different way. By staying in the present moment without getting hooked by any single thought, feeling, or sensation, we allow all to flow naturally. You might say, "That sounds easy, but how do I stop the 'getting hooked' part when I feel so devastated?"

Let's start with the understanding that mindfulness is a practice because you can't turn it on and off like a light switch. It's more of a muscle that has to be exercised to grow strong. You'll begin practicing some classic mindfulness exercises when you reach the end of this day. The idea is to stay in the moment and to observe your experience with curiosity, as if someone handed you 3-D glasses in your favorite movie theater. The movie has started. Scenes are flashing before your eyes. People, animals, airplanes, cars… you're so absorbed by the action you forget it's just images spliced together. Suddenly a glass shatters on screen and the fragments come flying toward your face, your hands instinctively go up to cover your eyes, but then you remember, it's only a movie. No scary scene will persist if you let the story unfold without stopping the projector.

In your real life practice, instead of thinking, "Oh no, here's the sadness again. I can't stand this," you acknowledge the feeling by keeping a fragment of that sentence: "Here's the sadness." Or you can be curious and nonjudgmental about the emotion by asking, "What could this be?"

If your mind reflexively answers, "It's sadness, stupid!" instead of getting hooked by either the sensation of "sadness" or the label "stupid," you can respond by staying in the moment without judgment. You could say, "There's anger and there's sadness." The idea is that instead of nursing any single thought or feeling, you come back to the present moment. You do that by being grounded through your senses, keeping in touch with the sights, sounds, smells, and textures around you or simply observing the rhythm of your breathing. It's like letting the carousel of emotions spin by while you watch the whole scene: the parents waving to their kids as they go round… the kids eating cotton candy, the smell of popcorn, the sounds of circus music. There's so much more going on than those emotions spinning by.

Case Study: Ben's Mindfulness

Ben was two months separated and three weeks into ACT therapy. He decided to try his hand at mindfulness practice. He set his timer for three minutes because that was all the time he could commit to sitting quietly with his feelings. Ben normally does things to get his mind off his problems; he likes to work on cars and anything mechanical. After his practice, he came back to therapy to report on his progress.

Ben: I tried doing that meditation thing.

Elaine: How did it go?

Ben: It felt stupid. I sat out on my balcony and watched cars go by… listened to an ambulance… heard a car alarm go off ... kids yelling, laughing. Then I started thinking about my wife and how she screwed me over, took my kids and my money. I could feel myself breathing hard, my whole body tensing up. I tried asking myself, "What might this feeling be?" like you told me, but it felt stupid because I knew *exactly* what it was. Pissed off. But, the funny thing is, my mind switched it up. It wasn't me feeling angry. I was a mechanic looking at an engine that was making a weird kind of noise. So I asked myself, "Where's this noise coming from?" It was coming from my life being turned upside down. Then I remembered what you told me about not getting hooked on any one thought and I went back to listening and breathing. I smelled tomato sauce coming from my neighbor's window. I noticed my stomach growling, and I felt hungry… then my timer went off.

Ben used an important principle during his mindfulness practice: He refused to engage in a struggle with his feelings—he did not get hooked by any single thought or emotion. When he felt himself getting stuck, he turned his attention back to his present awareness.

One might argue that the reason Ben enjoys working on cars is because it's a real-life mindfulness practice. A good mechanic has to start with a curious mind. What might be causing this rough idle? He looks at the engine, listens for sounds of distress, feels the parts with his hands—all in real time. He gets feedback as he makes changes and continues observing. You don't have to sit crossed-legged in a Zen pose with your thumb and forefinger touching to practice mindfulness. In fact, the more you do it as part of your everyday life, the easier it will be to establish the habit.

Paradoxically, by strengthening your tolerance to change, your life will take on greater stability. It's like being able to change the direction of your sails as you navigate the ocean. When winds are blowing hard, it's better to adjust the sails so that the wind becomes your ally. Not only will you get to your destination faster, there's less chance of getting battered along the way.

There's another mindfulness exercise in which you imagine placing your thoughts on leaves that are floating on a stream. When you notice yourself getting stuck on one particular thought, you mentally place the thought on one of the leaves floating by. The idea is to practice so that you become more comfortable with the act of observing and letting go of thoughts, feelings, or sensations that disturb you. You can do this with clouds, waves, puffs of smoke, birds flying off into the horizon—anything that passes by without necessarily stopping.

Remember that all kinds of thoughts and feelings are going to surface while you practice mindfulness. The trick is to keep bringing yourself back to what's happening around you and staying curious about everything that passes through your awareness. If you're still stumped about how to stay in the moment, find a dog. Dogs don't need to practice mindfulness—they are mindfulness in action. They constantly sniff, observe, listen, and lick the things around them. They don't stay with any one thing for very long unless it has to do with eating, playing, or sleeping. A dog that's scolded or even swatted by its master won't sit there and stew over it. In fact, as long as it isn't beaten or tortured, a dog will run straight to its master after a scolding, tail wagging, ready for the next adventure. Dogs bark at passing strangers but most stop barking once the coast is clear. They don't hold grudges and don't expect others to. Dogs are great at showing compassion. I've seen dogs that can sense their owner's sadness. They sit right by their master's side, "doggedly" staying in place to make sure they're okay.

Dogs are not as complicated as humans, but we can learn a lot from them about staying in the moment, remaining curious, and not holding on to any single emotion beyond our curiosity. Our ability to remember the past and imagine the future makes us uniquely human, but at a cost. We get stuck in our mental world of planning, worrying, nursing past injuries, and holding on to anger.

With all this talk of mindfulness, you might be tempted to think that it means pushing aside your emotions so they can go away and not bother you. Don't make that mistake. We've talked a lot about how important it is to accept your painful feelings so they don't turn into suffering. Accepting your sadness, anger, jealousy, or whatever feeling comes up, means acknowledging the emotion, feeling it, and just like Ben, the mechanic, using it to realize that there's something happening to upset the balance of your life. You've lost someone important to you. There is pain, but there is also growth. The important thing to remember for all these painful emotions is that overcoming requires accepting the pain, detaching from illusions (like possessing lovers), yielding to change without judging its impact on your future, and taking control of the things you can control in your life.

Below are some practices for staying in the moment while doing daily activities.

Exercise: Mindful Breathing

Dedicate three to five minutes (you can set a timer like Ben did) to practice mindfulness. Just relax and simply meditate by focusing on your breath. Breath naturally. If you find yourself getting hooked on any single thought, use it as an opportunity to practice coming back to the moment.

Let's say you think about your ex during this meditation. Your mind might wander into thoughts about how unfairly you've been treated or how you'll always be alone. Expect this to happen because your mind is still trying to solve the problem of divorce. Also, you're still grieving. When this happens, imagine making space for whatever upsetting thought or emotion surfaces. You can do this in several ways:

- ☯ Take a deep breath. As your chest expands, imagine that it is making space for the thought or the feeling it produces
- ☯ Imagine you're a great social justice warrior like Gandhi, the Buddha, or Jesus, and picture how they would respond to injustice by opening their heart to the opposition or turning the other cheek
- ☯ Place the thought or emotion in a bubble and watch it float away
- ☯ Picture the cells of your body expanding to make room for the upsetting thought with the acceptance that it's already there

When in doubt or feeling stumped, anchor your attention back to your breath. Don't try to change your breathing pattern, to slow it down or force it to be any way but what it is. These exercises are all about accepting not directing.

Exercise: Everyday Mindfulness

Here are some more mindfulness techniques that you can practice while you're doing day-to-day activities to strengthen the new habit:

Washing the Dishes: While you're washing the dishes, notice the water temperature. Feel how slippery things become when you add the dish soap. Smell the scent of the soap. As your fingers come in contact with the towel or sponge, note the texture—rough, smooth? Listen to the clinking and clattering sounds the plates and utensils make as you wash them.

Driving Home: Avoid the trance that blurs the scenery on your drive home by paying particular attention to the scenery: the landmarks, the trees, the color of the cars passing, the birds flying by in the sky. Listen to the sounds of traffic, the hum of your engine, the trucks rumbling down the road. Smell the scent of your car's interior or roll down the windows and breathe in the air. Squeeze the steering wheel and notice the impressions on your fingers. Wiggle your toes and observe the pressure your foot makes while pressing down on the gas.

Taking a Shower: Change the water temperature from time to time as you shower. Use a scrub brush or hand towel to get a different sensation as you soap up. If possible, use a scented soap or body scrub so you can breathe in the fragrance. Open your mouth wide under the shower and feel the pressure of the stream against your tongue, teeth and lips. Observe the spray of water and follow it as it transforms into rivulets that flow down your body. Listen to the thrumming or pulsing sounds surrounding you.

Mindful Eating: Hold a fig between your thumb and index finger. Feel its texture. Can you detect the ridges and crevices? Does it yield to pressure when you squeeze it? Bring it up to your nose and smell it. Can you tell it's a fig from the scent alone? Does it smell fruity or earthy? Now bring it up to your lips but don't place it in your mouth. Can you feel the grooves with just your lips? Does it feel dry or moist? Now place the fig in your mouth but don't chew. Take some time to explore the shape and crevices with your tongue. Are you salivating? Finally, bite down and chew slowly (at least 25 chews). Take in all the flavors as you break it down for swallowing.

This exercise has elicited some of the most intense reactions. Group members say things like, "I never knew a fig could taste so good," or "I can't believe I was missing all these intense flavors." Also, the practice of mindful eating is an excellent technique for weight loss because it slows down the pace of eating, giving the stomach time to sense that it's full.

Exercise: Mindful Cleaning for Your New Space

Now we're going to do a mindfulness exercise for letting go of some of the clutter that's no longer serving your needs. To bring mindfulness to the act of reorganizing your home after a breakup, it's important to frame the activity as a type of cleansing. This is an exercise in self-care. Focus on each activity instead of distracting yourself with television or phone conversations.

Take a mindful walk through your house in search of unneeded objects. Don't look at this as a type of relationship-building or -ending exercise. You're not trying to control anything, you're just making more space by letting go of attachments. Look for reasons to remove them from your life. Henry David Thoreau said, "That which you own, owns you." Free yourself with purpose. Look for things that drag you down either because of memories or the work it takes to keep them. Place those items in the trash, in a box to give to your ex, or a donation bag. Don't stop any emotion, even if some sentimental object makes you cry or feel despair. Remember, that what you resist, persists. Use radical acceptance to release strivings for things that are not under your control.

Day 5 Lessons:

- ☯ Mindfulness is an awareness of yourself and your environment without judgment or criticism
- ☯ Most feelings are repeats, but none stay for long unless they are fed and watered by your thoughts
- ☯ There is pain, but there is also growth

Day 6: Wise Mind

"Logic is the beginning of wisdom ... not the end."
—Mr. Spock, Star Trek

Do you notice that your mind will tell you one thing while your emotions say the opposite?

Mind: I've got to lose weight.

Emotions: I'm hungry.

Or

Mind: Let it go. Move on. You've stayed in this pit for way too long.

Emotions: But I can't live without him.

Your mind already has the right plan. So why can't your emotions just straighten up and get with the program?

Society places great stock in logic, to the exclusion of emotion. We use strategies that require us to identify the problem, gather the facts, review the data, and integrate all the information to devise an effective solution. If you remember Spock, from Star Trek, you may recall that he considered emotions to be "illogical" and distracting from the work at hand.

Our intellect is a treasure of towering marble cultivated in schools and universities. Emotions are the fluff. Friends take us out to drink or eat our sadness away. Parents and other loved ones kiss our wounds to "make it all better." The only cultivation our emotions get is the digging we do to bury them underground. Supporters mean well, but so much non-acceptance of pain sends the message that pain is to be avoided and there begins the road to suffering.

What if there was another way to mend the split between your mind and heart? You could start by throwing out the social programing and adding a seat for all that messy energy your emotions bring to the table. Think of it as brainstorming, where stakeholders try to solve a problem by tossing out ideas without anyone judging their quality until something clicks. A couple of ideas get connected and everyone agrees: "That's brilliant!" Wise Mind is brainstorming at a table for one. It's a tool for extracting the ideas your yin and yang are shouting out to solve your problem. Think of it as the "gut instinct" because the solution is already there, you just need to listen without judging. You know it's right when the answer releases that tightness in your chest. The reverse is also true. When you exclude one in favor of the other, say giving into your emotions with no consideration for your logic, it's that stomach-in-a-knot feeling you get when you know something's not right.

Let's look at an example from a therapy session to see how Wise Mind helps us understand the seesaw between thoughts and emotions.

Case Study: Paul Discovers His Wise Mind

Paul: I feel like I'm getting jerked around. And I'm doing it to myself. One minute I'm like, screw it, she's not worth it, I don't need this shit. The next minute I tell myself I just need to hear her voice. This can't be happening. I just want all this to stop!

Elaine: So it's like your mind is telling you to let go and your heart is telling you to give it one more shot.

Paul: Yeah. Exactly. But this heart thing is all bullshit because I've tried giving it one more shot so many times, and all she does is slam the door in my face.

Elaine: It sounds like you're ready to trash your feelings because they've led you down the wrong path—trying to get Sophie to take you back. And that hasn't worked.

Paul: True that.

Elaine: So now it's a battle between what your mind says about moving on and what your heart says about not giving up. That must be hard, I mean, living with that struggle every day.

Paul: It's friggin' driving me crazy.

Elaine: Let's try something. It's called Wise Mind. I want you to imagine that right now your thoughts are on a pedestal. When you listen to them, you tell yourself you've got it right. Now, let's put your feelings down here on this footstool because they don't deserve to be as high up there as your thoughts. You might even picture yourself tripping over the footstool because it gets in your way while you're trying to do what your thoughts are telling you to do. Can you picture that?

Paul: Yeah, I got it.

Elaine: Now imagine that you take your thoughts off the pedestal and your emotions off the footstool, and you place both of them on a table—side by side. Neither is higher than the other and neither one has more value than the other. They're both here with important information for you. Can you do that?"

Paul: Yeah.

Elaine: So let's listen to your thoughts without judging. What are they saying?

Paul: They're saying, "Sophie told you she wants out. She doesn't want to be with you. She has a boyfriend. What else does she have to do, slap you over the head with a two-by-four? Don't you get it? She doesn't want you anymore. Move on, man. Show some dignity."

Elaine: Okay, good. Your thoughts are saying that the data screams that you should be letting go of the relationship with Sophie because it's clear that she doesn't want to be with you. That holding on is hopeless and will only lower your self-respect.

Paul: Correct.

Elaine: Now let's listen to your feelings and remember, the message they're going to offer you is at the same level as what your mind is saying. What are they saying?

Paul: Okay, okay… my feelings are saying, "You guys were meant to be together. Just because she's got a boyfriend doesn't mean you can't win her back. Don't be a wuss. Don't give up so easy. You know you miss her. You know she's the only one you want. Do whatever it takes to get her back."

Elaine: Excellent! Both your mind and your heart are making some really strong arguments for doing the opposite thing. Or at least that's what it sounds like.

Paul: Seriously.

Elaine: Okay, this is where it gets fun. We're going to use Wise Mind to reach a decision about how to move forward. I want you to think of Wise Mind as the referee that listens to both sides and then makes the right call. Since both your mind and your heart are a part of you, it's going to feel right when you strike a balance between them because it won't feel like a tug-of-war inside.

Paul: Hey, if I could do that, I would've done it already.

Elaine: I understand. But before, you were caught in a battle between the two of them, thinking that your thoughts were right and your emotions were wrong… that you were weak when you gave in to your feelings. Now you're listening to both of them with compassion. You're giving both of them equal value and equal time. That's what makes the difference. Let's just try it and see what happens.

Paul: Okay. So if I got this right, I would say my thoughts are saying it's better to let her go, and my feelings are saying I've got to get her back. But really, I don't have any control over getting her back. Believe me, I've tried. So I still gotta go with my mind and let her go.

Elaine: Let's say you do that. Does it feel right in your gut? Do your feelings tell you that's the way to go?

Paul: No. That's what's driving me crazy.

Elaine: You're breaking it down into what you have and don't have control over. That helps. You said you haven't been able to control her because every time you've tried, she shuts you down. So what do you have control over?

Paul: I have no control over her. But I guess I have control over me. [Paul smirks] But not that much.

Elaine: Okay, let's use whatever control you have. Let's listen to your mind saying, "Move on." And let's listen to your heart saying, "Hold on." How can you put that together?

Paul: I guess I could tell myself that she could do whatever she wants. I'm gonna live my life like my mind says, but I don't have to give up on her like my heart says. Yeah—maybe I could tell her, "Hey Sophie, I get the fact that you don't want to be with me, and you can do whatever you want, but I still love you and I haven't given up on us."

Elaine: How does that feel when you say it?

Paul: It feels like… kind of nice… like it's this middle where I don't have to completely give up, but I don't have to keep begging her to stay like some wimp. I guess it's not so awful if I hold on a little longer, as long as I don't try to force her into doing something she doesn't want.

Elaine: I'd say that's a perfect call by your Wise Mind, your referee. It gives you the freedom to take your time. It respects the fact that you still care for Sophie, and it reminds you that she still has the right to choose what she wants. Most importantly, it breaks up the war going on inside you.

Paul: Yeah, you're right. I can feel it.

Exercise: Wise Mind

Wise Mind teaches us to value our wholeness, cultivating the *holiness* that exists within each of us, waiting to be discovered. Both of our eyes see the world from slightly different perspectives, both in service of the whole: you. Without both eyes, you lose depth perception and your vision becomes flat. The same thing happens with your thoughts and feelings; listening to one and ignoring the other makes your reactions flat and limited.

Today you're going to practice a Wise Mind exercise to explore your gut instinct. We saw Wise Mind in action with Paul trying to reconcile his thoughts and feelings toward Sophie. He decided that he could let Sophie live her life while he made his own choices about how to go on with his life. This gut instinct solution exists in you too. All you have to do is tap into it. You'll be surprised by the things your Wise Mind comes up with when you engage it.

Construct some Wise Mind scenarios between what your intellect and your emotions are telling you about your relationship. It could be the big battle between your mind telling you to let go of your ex and your feelings saying to hold on. It could be something as simple as deciding to throw something of your ex's away versus throwing it in their face. If you're unsure of how to go about setting up your own Wise Mind scenario, go back to Paul's example for guidance. Explore at least one scenario in which you can practice Wise Mind.

Scenario:	Mind says:	Heart says:	Wise Mind says:

Day 6 Lessons:

- ☯ You will make the right call by listening to both your logic and your emotions
- ☯ Wise Mind teaches us to value our wholeness

Day 7: Values and Goals

"You never know what worse luck your bad luck has saved you from."—Cormac McCarthy

For most of us, divorce feels like we've been cheated out of happiness. Finances get tight and the buck stops with you. You take care of the car, you cook the meals, you do the wash, you pay the rent. Life is already demanding enough: How are you supposed to find the energy to set a new course for life? It's like saving for retirement. You tell yourself, "I'll start next month." But the bills keep coming and before you can say, "Charge it," the money is gone.

ACT therapists point out that we're trading control of our lives for control of our feelings. The trade means we toss our aspirations into the back seat so our mind can steer away from the pain. This "experiential avoidance" can stand in the way of our goals and values. It's another way of describing the non-acceptance that creates suffering.

Your life has been immersed in a new reality that you can learn to respond to if you're willing. It doesn't mean you approve or agree with the divorce, or how it unfolds. But approve or not, the breakup is already happening. It's time to get behind the wheel with a map.

First, you need to know where you're going.

Quick Self-check:

Are you saying the word "divorce" out loud?

☯ "No, I won't be with Jim at the party, we're getting divorced."

☯ "I'm in the middle of a divorce, that's why we're selling the house."

☯ "I didn't ask for the divorce, but it is what it is."

☯ "That's true; I didn't mention the divorce before, it was too hard for me to accept."

What do you hear in these statements? Announcing your divorce is like throwing the doors open and inviting people into your house after a hurricane. You may still be walking on shattered glass and soaked carpeting but the clean-up is a beginning, and it gets easier with help.

On this, your last day of formal lessons, we will use all your exercises to construct a compass for the rest of your journey. Do you feel a twinge of fear? Maybe there is a bit of excitement peeking out from under the water-soaked couch in your living room. The storm of splitting up has taken its toll, but it has also wiped the slate. How do you want to furnish your new home? The question calls on you to think of your values. What's important for your life? You can put the furniture wherever you want without asking, without forcing it to conform to your marriage. In the Myths chapter, we looked at your sacrifices, all those things you gave up to nurture and grow your relationship. Your love's labor sanctified your marriage. Now it's time to sanctify your life by deciding what you need to discover. Your new life is waiting for you like a brilliant sunrise on the day after a tempest.

When Joe and I walked the Camino de Santiago, a pilgrimage route through Northern Spain, I met a woman we called Denise, who was going through a divorce. She was still mourning over her loss, but she decided to challenge herself by walking the 500-mile distance between St. Jean Pied de Port in France and Santiago de Compostela, Spain. While she walked the path, she wrote poetry and posted it on her website. She developed a following, and it spurred her to keep writing. Here are a few pages from our book, *In Movement There Is Peace*, to give you a snapshot of how one person took the wheel.

Denise and I had some time alone on the trek into Ponferrada. It was an informal walking therapy. She described how she had married at twenty-one and raised a beautiful daughter with Sam, her husband. They both worked hard to establish his practice as a plastic surgeon in San Francisco: a place where people refuse to grow old, where sixty is the new thirty, and gray is the new platinum. She described her soon-to-be ex-husband as intelligent and prominent in their community. Her daughter attends an Ivy League school and seems destined for a life of distinction. Denise was joyriding the American dream for her 5th straight decade, up until a set of steel spikes punctured the tires: her husband had fallen in love with a young student at the college where Denise taught as a professor.

Sam wanted no part of marital therapy and had already filed for divorce. At the time, the whole thing came as a shock. "This isn't supposed to happen. He promised to stay forever, it's in the marriage vows, 'till death do us part!'" Denise was stunned by her husband's resolve. No matter what she did, no matter how she pleaded or how she pushed for counter-offers, he refused to budge. It was as if he had already worked it all out in his mind and was just showing her the divorce papers as an afterthought. "He was so cold. I never saw him like that before." She couldn't stop the rush of memories and raw emotions once she started. "He said he loved me but wasn't 'in love' with me anymore. What the hell is that supposed to mean? Isn't love just love? How did he stop loving me? I can't imagine not loving him anymore."

It's hard to listen to the kind of anguish Denise is feeling without trying to do some kind of therapy, even if it's on a mountain in the middle of nowhere. It didn't really matter whether we were sitting in my office or in a sleepy town in Spain. The pain was the same. "Denise, if I could share only one piece of advice with you at a time like this, when you think you'll never get over this indescribable pain, it's this: your husband is giving you what you need, not what you want."

I could tell this made absolutely no sense to her. Her face showed what she was too polite to say in words: "What the heck does that mean?" I expected this reaction because I get it every time I use it in divorce therapy. Every person who resists the breakup of their marriage will tell you what they need is to stay married, and therein lies the paradox. The truth is, they want to stay married. They want the familiar comfort of being in a steady and secure marriage with the person they love. But many of these same individuals had stopped asking themselves what they needed years ago. Denise was a great example. After the initial shock of hearing the needs versus wants explanation, she warmed up to the idea, and that gave me the courage to ask a very personal question: "What have you been missing in your life with your husband?"

Her answer came in fits and starts, but it could all be distilled down to the one answer that brought tears to her eyes: "I gave up my dream to be a writer in order to support his practice." The light was starting to go on; I could see it in her eyes. She was picking up on the distinction between "need" versus "want." She said, "Sam told me 'art doesn't pay' and he had some pretty huge medical school loans. So, of course, the practice had to take priority. I took a little part-time job at the college so I could have more time to work as his office manager. I got an education in accounting, but I didn't need that. I needed – no: I need self-expression."

Since she'd started the Camino, Denise had been writing poetry every day: "Even if it's just a couple of minutes during a rest break, or right after something moves me, like a bird singing 'hello' just for me." She described how the pain and poetry were breaking through a wall that had separated her from her creativity. The one time she beamed with pride aside from talking about her daughter's accomplishments was when she described her sister Kate's review of her poetry: "She calls them masterpieces."

"Now we're talking!" I encouraged as I realized she understood the concept of getting what she needed. Denise could feel it too. She quickly offered more information: "Even my

daughter said, 'Mom, you're like a new person. You seem happy for the first time in a long time.' I didn't get it at the time because I couldn't imagine myself happy without my husband, but I think I know what she means." Denise couldn't stop. She had latched on and refused to let go: "I even lost fifty pounds, and my doctor said this was great because I was pre-hypertensive and he was afraid I would have to start medicine if my blood pressure kept rising."

I quickly chimed in: "We call it the 'divorce diet' because it's so common for people to lose their appetite when they first separate."

It was impossible to miss the glimmer in Denise's eyes when she added, "Even this trip here...this Camino, is something I dreamed about for years, but there was always a reason why I couldn't leave. It was never the right time for his practice. Now I'm here, and I can't believe I'm almost done!"

It was easy to see how much the Camino had boosted Denise's confidence. The path had also become devotional for her: "My husband was never a spiritual man, and I gave up practicing my faith when we got married because he convinced me it was a waste of time. Now that I'm alone, I attend Mass every opportunity I get, and the more I speak to God, the more I realize I'm never really alone."

And it wasn't just the spiritual company. Denise had a sizable following as she documented her daily adventures on her blog: "It feels so good to have people reading and spurring me on...I can tell they are really getting into it. It's almost like they are traveling here beside me."

By the time we reached the Templar Castle in Ponferrada, it was clear that Denise was already immersed in the bitter-sweetness of her experience. She wasn't so outraged by the idea that she was deriving some benefit from her breakup. She could see the needs she'd been denying herself. No doubt, she still wanted her husband back, but she could see, far off in the distance – past Compostela, that there was a woman waiting for her attention. A woman she had neglected for years and was just starting to get reacquainted with. It was the woman her husband had discarded, ignorant of the wealth he was losing, like some long-lost piece of art discovered at a yard sale, invaluable but carelessly abandoned.

Exercise: Following Your Values and Goals

What's important to you? Forget about what your mother, your father, your ex, or even society tells you should be important. This is only about you and what you think. There are many dimensions of your life that you may have neglected in service of your relationship.

- ☯ List some places you want to go or sights you want to see.

____

____

____

- ☯ Is spirituality important to you? How would you tap into that dimension of your life?

____

____

____

- ☯ Are there people you value deeply but haven't been paying attention to? Who are they and how would you reconnect?

____

____

____

- What about your career? Is it time for a change? What kind?

____

____

____

- Have you taken your education as far as you would like? Write down a degree or certification you would like to achieve.

____

____

____

- What kind of legacy do you want to leave behind? How do you want people to remember you?

____

____

____

In my practice, I like to use a technique to reduce experiential avoidance. The exercise will help you approach (instead of avoiding) the detour your life has taken. It's called the "Six Months Left to Live Plan."

Imagine your doctor has just told you that you have six months to live, your condition is terminal and there's no cure.

You say, "What? There must be something, some treatment I can try."

"I'm sorry, it's inoperable. There's nothing we can do."

At first, you're in shock. Six months? You go through the stages of grief at lightning speed.

Denial: "This can't be happening."

Bargaining: "There must be something I can do… alternative medicines, experimental treatments. I'll try ANYTHING!"

Anger: "You're a horrible doctor. I'll sue!"

Depression: "Why me? It's useless. There's nothing for me to do but curl up in a ball and wait to die."

Acceptance: "Everybody dies, not everyone lives."

So you get past the raw, bloodcurdling fear, and now you're left with some important decisions. You know you can't take it with you. Even the separation takes on a different feel because you'll soon be separated from all your attachments. These six months are going to go fast. What will you do with the time you have left?

Case Study: Dan Has Six Months to Live

Dan was still grieving the loss of his family. Every time he'd make dinner to prove to his wife that he'd changed, she'd leave him with the same caution: "Just because we ate together doesn't mean I'm coming back—I'm only doing this for the girls."

Dan was living in his single-guy apartment, feeling unhappy.

I asked during one of our sessions, "What would you do if you knew you had six months to live?"

At first, he was surprised by the question. He fumbled with his thoughts.

"Maybe dying wouldn't be so bad… I've got nothing to live for right now."

I decided to give him some more time, he was still too depressed. After a few more weeks of therapy and an antidepressant, his mood began to brighten and he brought up the topic himself.

"I've been thinking about what you asked me, about what I'd do if I had six months to live. I've always wanted to build a bass guitar."

"Really? That's awesome," I said. "What's stopping you?"

"I don't have any room in my apartment. It's just got the one bedroom, and it's already packed with stuff."

"Is there any other room you could use?"

"I have a small dining area. It's really part of the kitchen, but still, that's for my family—it's where we eat together."

We talked more about how saving that space for the family was his clinging attachment, his way of holding on despite his wife's reminders to stop expecting her to come back. That attachment to his dining room was his lifeline. The six-month scenario I'd proposed gave him a new time frame for cutting the cord. He took the assignment seriously and pretended that his life was going to end in six months.

"I guess I could always put the furniture in storage and open that space up for building my bass guitar. I mean, if I only have six months to live, I wouldn't want a bunch of chairs and a table to stop me. In fact, I could just get rid of the chairs and use the table as my workspace."

"Who knows," I said. "It could give the kids something to get excited about."

In the next session Dan explained how he'd emptied out his dining room and set up all the woodworking tools and supplies he needed to build his bass guitar. When his wife and kids came to visit, she was shocked. He relayed the events of the day during our next session.

"She asked me, 'What are you doing… where are we supposed to eat?' I looked her straight in the eye and answered, 'We're going to sit on the floor and have a picnic.'"

He told her about his lifelong dream of building a bass guitar. Then he made dinner. He and the kids were so excited about his project; they didn't care that they were eating on the floor.

A month later, during another therapy session, Dan described how he was playing his bass guitar in the storage shed he'd rented for his excess furniture.

"Some guys were putting stuff in another storage room and they heard me playing. The lead guy wanted to know if I'd play with them and I said, 'Hell yeah!' We did it and it worked out great. They asked me to join them as a regular. The group isn't famous or anything, but I'm playing in a real band! We play Fleetwood Mac and the Beatles. Who would've thought… I feel so pumped. I haven't felt this good in forever."

Dan continued playing on weekends and by our next session, he was complaining about how tired he felt when he picked up the girls for his weekly visitation.

"Leigh asked me, 'What's wrong with you?' and I told her that I was playing with the band the night before and it went later than I expected."

With Dan feeling more in control, our therapy sessions were spread out. It was two months later when he came back for his next appointment.

"Something strange happened last weekend. I'd been wanting to visit the Vietnam Memorial in DC for years, but I always put it off. There were too many responsibilities, too many things on the "Honey-do" list. This last weekend I wasn't playing with the band, so I just took off—on a whim. I decided it was one of the things on my bucket list that I had to see before I die."

"How was it?" I asked.

"It was the best thing that ever happened to me. You'll never guess. I was standing there with tears in my eyes, thinking about all the soldiers who gave their lives, feeling the letters of their names carved in the stone beneath my fingertips. Then my phone went off. I thought about ignoring it, but I noticed it was 'Keep It Short & Sweet', so I answered. You know what she said? She said, 'I can hear people in the background. Where are you?'"

"What did you tell her?"

"I told her the truth. I said, 'I'm in DC at the Vietnam Memorial.' She asked, 'Why would you go there?' You know what I said?"

"What?"

Dan smiled so big the corners of his mouth almost touched the corners of his ears.

"I said, 'Because I can.'"

"What did she say to that?"

"That's the wildest part of the whole thing. She said, 'You liar! You're with someone. You're seeing another woman. You would never go somewhere like that alone.' The funny thing is, she was right. Before I started this death-in-six-months thing, I would never have taken a trip like that by myself. After I convinced her that I wasn't seeing another woman, that I was living out a dream of mine, she said she wanted to talk. Just the two of us."

Dan met with Leigh a few days later and learned that his weekend trip had raised her own fears of losing him. Dan and his wife kept talking and later on, started dating. He placed no expectations on her because he understood the concept of attachments. She didn't belong to him. She was an individual with her own dreams and desires. He told me it was fun to start new and this time he was the one enjoying the freedom of no expectations.

Dan had started living his life according to his values and the goals he created for his bucket list. Living a purposeful life and accepting his pain made him stronger. The people around him noticed, especially the woman who knew him best.

Have you ever heard of rapprochement? When a baby is born, they don't recognize the boundary between mother and self. It's attachment in its purest form. It's not Mama and baby—there is only the one. As the weeks and months go by, the infant starts staring at their hands, flexing fingers and watching how things work. They're just beginning to grasp the idea of separateness.

As the baby grows into a toddler, they learn to walk and face the challenge of exploration. Standing on these awesome devices we call legs, they waddle from one room to another, striking out on a path away from mother. But make no mistake—in the beginning, they won't go far. In fact, they won't go farther than visual distance from Mom. If she's too far away, they stop, feeling insecure with their separation. But, as long as they can see Mom, they're unstoppable.

Observe how both you and your ex engage in the dance of rapprochement. You might feel compelled to call about a bill that came in unexpectedly. Or maybe you make an unannounced visit to the house just to pick up some clothes or forgotten keys. It happens without awareness. The message behind the actions is: "I need to know you're still there."

Watch for this behavior. If you see it in yourself, recognize this need, but don't judge it. Work to fill your rapprochement needs in other ways. The toddler might not explore if they don't see their mother, but they might take a chance if they see a big, red balloon bouncing up ahead. Doing things that you find personally satisfying will help.

Today's practice will guide you past your relationship needs and focus on your life needs. Let's go back to Dan. He had an assignment to pretend he had six months to live. With the short time left, he had to set priorities by examining his values. With death staring him in the face, the choice was simple. He decided that he valued creativity. Isn't it interesting how accepting our limited existence can strip away the day-to-day demands and reveal the core?

James Patterson said, "The funny thing about facing imminent death is that it really snaps everything else into perspective." It reminds us that our attachments are illusions. No matter how hard we try, we just can't take it with us.

Building a guitar, joining a band, and taking a trip to a place on his bucket list revealed Dan's priorities. Those three activities were focused on his passion for creativity. How ironic that Dan's decision to focus on his artistic expression had such a positive impact on his relationship with his wife.

A Zen poem captures his experience:

"Go to the edge," the voice said.
"No!" they said. "We will fall."
"Go to the edge," the voice said.
"No!" They said. "We will be pushed over."
"Go to the edge," the voice said.
So they went. And they were pushed. And they flew.
- Anonymous

Now it's your turn. What will you do to make the next six months meaningful?

Exercise: Six Months To Live

Imagine you have six months to live. Let's first look at what's important to you by prioritizing your values. Many different dimensions of life can be important. You will need to decide which comes first, second, third, and so on. On the form below prioritize the values in your life in rank order from 1–11. Then, in the right column, enter the amount of time you're currently engaging in those activities.

Rank	Topic	% doing things related to this value
	Family: Spending time with your parents, grandparents, siblings, cousins, aunts, uncles, nieces, nephews.	
	Friends: Taking time with people who are nurturing.	
	Children: Having fun with your children while teaching values and modeling positive behaviors.	
	Charity: Sharing with community in a way that makes the world better.	
	Work: Cultivating your career, mentoring employees, making the workplace more fulfilling.	
	Religion/Spirituality: Growing in faith, praying, reading a spiritual book, joining in fellowship.	
	Money: Establishing a workable budget, studying investment options to promote wealth, and investing in regular incrcments.	
	Health: Establishing healthy habits by seeing your doctor regularly, watching your diet, not smoking, getting proper rest, and exercising regularly.	
	Creativity: Expressing creativity through painting, playing an instrument, pottery, poetry, dancing, or any other form of self-expression.	
	Romance: Having someone special to be intimate with, including sexually, for expression of romantic love.	
	Sexuality: Healthy outlets for sexual release (e.g., masturbation or intercourse)	

Once you've ranked your values, check to see how much you're engaging in them. For instance, if you've ranked your children as #1, ask yourself, "What percentage of my time am I devoting to my kids beyond making and eating meals, brushing teeth, and bath time." Just as importantly, are you asking for help from others for the good of your children? Some people let their embarrassment or fear of imposing on others keep them from asking for help. But if you ranked your children as #1, you'll get closer to your goal by pushing past the fear and asking anyway. If you've ranked your religion or spirituality as #1, ask yourself how much time you're devoting to your fellowship, to living a life based on your faith, or to accepting things as they unfold in your life as part of God's perfect plan.

There is one important exception that relates to romance and sexual intercourse that has already been addressed in our section on the deadly rebound. You can keep romance and intercourse within your values framework, but engaging in them before you're emotionally ready may cause you to go backward instead of forward.

If you notice a discrepancy between your values and the time you spend on activities related to them, it's time to create a list of goals to close the gap. In the table below, list your top three values and specific, achievable goals associated with them. Strive to make your behavior match up with your values and goals.

	Value	**Specific Goal to Align Behavior with Value**
Ex:	*Health*	*Work out 3 times a week for the next 4 weeks.*
1		
2		
3		

Exercise: My Bucket List

Answer the following questions realistically, with something you can do right now. You don't have to climb Mount Everest, but whatever you do, keep it consistent with your values.

Write down the Month, Day and Year six months from today.

DATE ________________

Next, complete the bucket list prompts below:

Identify three bucket-list activities you want to do.

1. ______________________________
2. ______________________________
3. ______________________________

Identify three things you want to learn how to do.

1. ______________________________
2. ______________________________
3. ______________________________

Identify three positive impacts you can have on someone (other than your ex).

1. ______________________________
2. ______________________________
3. ______________________________

If you feel stumped, think back to when you were a child. What did you love to do? You know yourself better than anyone else. Listen to that soft-hearted, little rascal who had independent dreams before getting married. Make a decision to nurture your innocence and curiosity.

Now take a look at your calendar and assign a hard date next to each of your answers. Commit to the dates and activities. Start by making them realistic and doable.

You will be surprised at the opportunities that come your way when you break through the bars society has created in your mind. Even if you think your future is doomed, make a commitment to live this day without judgment— tell yourself that you have no way of knowing how an event will unfold. Little miracles will bloom in your daily affairs and they're just hints of the greater life waiting for you.

Day 7 Lessons:

- ☯ Our attachments are illusions
- ☯ Make your behavior consistent with your goals and values

Chapter 9. What Dan Did Right

We've followed Dan throughout this book and seen how, despite his grief, he learned to have fun in the ocean without Leigh. Instead of trying to pull her in his direction, he went out and practiced life without clinging attachment or judgment.

Here are some key things Dan did to rediscover his joy:

1. Dan didn't rush into a divorce.

Many couples push for a quick resolution to stop the pain. It's as if they want to rip the Band-Aid off quickly to get it over with. When Dan received the divorce papers from Leigh, he avoided the temptation to sign them right away. He left them laying on his counter as a reminder that the relationship needed to change.

All things being equal, it's best to engage in "benign neglect" when it comes to immediate divorce. That doesn't mean ignoring your ex's demands. It does mean taking control over your actions and staying close to the middle ground. The middle ground means no extremes—neither a quick divorce nor a quick reconciliation. Think of it as staying centered.

2. Dan asked for help instead of trying to solve the problem alone.

Dan had been separated for a month when he walked into our Divorce Recovery class. His friend urged him to attend and he followed through on the advice. Dan didn't know if a group was his thing, but he knew his emotions were too shaky to go it alone.

There are many directions to take when seeking help: clergy, therapists, support groups, outreach clinics, online forums, and chat rooms. The important thing is to find a person or group that understands your needs. Our group helped Dan uncover the truth: He is whole apart from his marriage.

Dan pinned a sticky note over his computer: "If you always do what you always did, you'll always get what you always got." Allow someone supportive to help you establish new, positive behaviors to enhance your growth during this transitional time.

3. Dan used radical acceptance to focus on the things he had control over and to let go of the things he had no control over.

Dan could have kept trying to change Leigh's mind. He could have worked harder to make dinners in his dedicated dining room, or pleaded for more chances. In short, he could have continued resisting. He wanted his marriage more than anything, even more than building a bass guitar or playing in a band. But during his therapy, he realized that even though he valued his relationship above all else, he could not directly control what Leigh did or what she thought of him. So he radically accepted the pain of his separation and everything changed; he stopped suffering. He also chose to hold on to his power by exerting effort on the things he still had control over.

Alcoholics Anonymous uses the Serenity Prayer to help millions of people discover new lives:

"God grant me the serenity to accept the things I cannot change;
the courage to change the things I can;
and the wisdom to know the difference."

Most psychologists will tell you that no one can control another person. That's only partially true. We are social beings, affected by those around us, whether purposeful or not. If someone stands too close to us in line, our natural response (in America) is to move to create space. Licking a spoon and handing it to someone with a germ phobia is a sure fire way to stop them from eating with that spoon. Examples of human action/reaction abound in everyday life. For Dan, giving up his resistance to the divorce resulted in dramatic changes. When he stopped trying to steer Leigh in his direction, he had more energy to blaze his own trail and Leigh gained more respect for him. Dr. Elisabeth Kübler-Ross said, "Learn to get in touch with the silence within yourself and know that everything in this life has a purpose, there are no mistakes, no coincidences, all events are blessings given to us to learn from." When Dan accepted the lessons of his life, the blessings abounded.

4. Dan recognized the truth of his mortality and focused on his goals and values.

Dan's bucket list based on the "Six Months Left to Live" exercise gave him the freedom to live according to his values and goals. Accepting himself as a unique and whole person, allowed Dan to see that his life was singular. His existence could not be tethered to any other human being just as birds can fly together in a flock but can't fly yoked together. I asked Dan during one of our sessions, "Which would you rather have on your epitaph—'He died wishing his wife would come back' or 'He lived a full and loving life'?"

We all have goals and values that help define our lives. For Dan, it was creativity. Despite being an engineer, he had an artist's soul. Perhaps Leigh could tell he wasn't happy. Perhaps she was challenging him, whether consciously or unconsciously, to express his creativity. Dan had a blast building his bass guitar, playing in a band, and traveling to DC. These were only some of the dreams he envisioned for his life. He dove into them because they represented a core value he'd been neglecting while pursuing his other dreams of building a family. It took guts for him to break away from his routine. He wasn't looking for a second career—he could barely concentrate on his primary job. With help, he placed one foot in front of the other, took a leap of faith, and a net appeared. You may believe that this kind of thing doesn't happen to regular people, but Dan is proof that it does. All it takes is that leap into your precious life.

5. Dan maintained his responsibilities as a parent.

Dan could have avoided his children and focused only on himself. Visiting his two daughters was a sore spot because it reminded him of the comfortable family life he lost. He felt sad every time he picked up his girls and every time he dropped them off. The reception from Leigh was like turning a corner in an unfamiliar neighborhood; he never knew what type of reception he'd get. Sometimes she was cold, sometimes neutral, and sometimes desperate for help. Other times she seemed happy to see him. He'd take a deep breath, knock on her door and strap in for the emotional roller coaster at every visit.

Many parents give up and stay away. They look for excuses to move, to stay busy, to avoid the pain. They aren't bad parents—they just don't know how to cope with their sadness and the changes divorce brings: "I've stopped going for visitation because it hurts too much. The kids are just going to forget about me anyway." While these thoughts may seem real, especially if your ex has started a new relationship, the truth is that your children will never forget you. If you stick it out, they will remember that you were there for them during a very confusing time in their lives. Dan's behavior sent a clear message: "My relationship with my children is more important than the pain that comes when we say goodbye."

> A word to the wise, if you're dealing with teenagers, all bets are off. They live in a labile world of emotions that will likely change once their brain fully matures. Don't follow their lead, even if they reject you. Follow your values so you can set the example. Remember that the opposite of love is not hate.

6. Dan stopped judging.

Dan stopped accusing Leigh of ruining his life. During the stressful experience of separation and divorce, emotions run hot. Dan felt confused, scared, and frequently betrayed, and that was just before breakfast. He wanted more than anything to get back what he'd lost. When Leigh kept telling him it was over, she became his target for anger and blame.

Through ACT, he learned that he was not going to be able to stop the pain, but he could stop suffering. He understood that blaming Leigh was a type of non-acceptance that was causing his suffering. Accepting the pain and the loss of his marriage placed Leigh and Dan on the same side of the table, looking across at the old, dead relationship staring back at them. They were no longer adversaries—they had both lost something.

Like the father in *The Man Without Judgment*, Dan decided he didn't know what impact the separation would ultimately have on his life. He kept his faith in a greater plan and developed his purposeful life.

7. Dan kept the lines of communication open while detaching and respected Leigh's right to choose.

Dan usually answered the phone when Leigh called. He used the concept of rapprochement—imagining Leigh as a toddler who was exploring the world but still afraid of going too far. He knew about the Leaver profiles. When they talked, he tried hard to keep their conversations short and to the point. He changed his wife's name on his cell phone to "Keep It Short & Sweet." He couldn't help smiling when the calls came in because Leigh is 5'1". Whenever she called, the contact name displayed on his phone painted a pleasant picture in his mind and reminded him to stay on topic. Sometimes, when he was too busy at work or didn't feel emotionally capable of talking to his struggling ex, he gave himself permission to let the call go to voicemail.

He reminded himself that Leigh was an individual and had a right to make choices, regardless of how it impacted him. He made a choice to keep his wedding band on but reminded himself the ring is a symbol of love, not a finger cuff. He admitted that it hurt when Leigh took hers off, but he realized his reaction was based on clinging attachment.

8. Dan stopped trying to get Leigh to change her mind.

Dan was no superhero. He tried everything he could think of to get Leigh back. He begged, bargained, slammed doors, cried, and threatened. But he realized that these non-accepting behaviors were making things worse. The more he tried to convince Leigh that he needed her, the more she resisted. Every time she saw him, all she could see was the next fight for survival. In Leigh's mind, she needed to push him away if she was to survive. His resistance led to her resistance, just like the troll and the dog fighting over the mutton shank at the beginning of our story. After dinner, when he would stare into her eyes, she could feel the struggle. His approach created a cue for her avoidance.

Dan started to realize that he got a lot more mileage out of family time when he focused on the present and exercised compassion toward everyone in the room. He still wanted her back, but he accepted the pain and stopped talking about how much it hurt to be apart. Ironically, the more he accepted the pain, the better he felt. He practiced making space for the things he would normally resist. He changed his focus to his own life, his own happiness. It was his way of saying, "If you're drowning, I have faith that you will regain your balance all by yourself."

9. Dan used Wise Mind to guide his actions.

Dan used Wise Mind to bridge the gap between his thoughts and his emotions. He listened to both sides. His intellect told him, "Don't sign the divorce papers. Do what it takes to get your family back." His emotions were looking for a geographical cure: "Sign the papers and move somewhere else, anywhere. Start a new life." Through Wise Mind, he discovered his solution. He did not sign the divorce papers, but he started his new life right in his little apartment. When Leigh would ask him why he hadn't signed the divorce papers, he let her know that he needed to do what he thought was right: "I'm not ready yet, Leigh, but I'm working on it. In the meantime, I understand you are ready."

10. Dan learned the difference between grief and depression.

We've devoted Appendix I at the end of this book to the critical difference between divorce grief and clinical depression. In short, grief is surmountable while clinical depression can perpetuate a cycle of hopelessness and helpless. When Dan was presented with the "Six Months to Live" scenario, his passive suicidal response sent a signal that his mood had plummeted past grief. The good news is the antidepressants we use today are much safer, better tolerated, and highly effective. Dan tried the most effective treatment for depression first: exercise. But when that and other behavioral strategies weren't enough, he supplemented his therapy with an antidepressant. Within a month, he was able to sleep better, had more energy, was more focused, and could shift his thoughts when memories of Leigh threatened to take him down. Some argue that mindfulness is incompatible with pharmaceutical drugs, but witnessing the impact in clinical practice is proof that meds and mindfulness are not mutually exclusive. Using an antidepressant with Dan was like standing beside a child learning to ride a bicycle. The medication kept him steady long enough for him to gain his own confidence.

11. Dan practiced mindfulness every day.

Dan turned bitterness into compassion by staying curious and in the moment, with love in his heart. It would have been easy for Dan to narrowly define love as romance. When Leigh withdrew affection, he could have given up on his chances for love and happiness. Instead, he made a point of staying in the moment and observing the events around him, resisting the impulse to dwell in the past or to force a future. Staying in the "now" allowed him to go to work and pay attention to his job. It allowed him to play his music in synchrony with the other band members. As a musician, he practiced mindfulness whenever he ran a finger over the smooth bass guitar built by his own hands. The weight felt good in his hands. He could appreciate the way it resonated with his voice when he sang.

When he played with his kids, he made a point to look into their eyes and hug them. He experimented with mindfulness practices by combing and braiding the girls' hair. The contact was good for all of them. It showed both Dan and the kids that they were loved and still lovable.

Dan did get that kitten after all. It was perhaps the best model for mindfulness. The cat taught him how to stay in the moment as she stalked a dust ball under the bed or lunged after a laser pointer. She purred with contentment snuggling on his chest at night. His bed didn’t feel so lonely with his new companion and she was happy to be there with him.

Chapter 10. Conclusion: Choosing L-O-V-E

You continue to climb the mountain and finally reach a small clearing on the top. You can see for miles in all directions and notice trails on the other side heading down in many different directions. You pause for a second to catch your breath and take your bearings. While brushing the dust from your pants you hear steps approaching from behind. Turning quickly, you see the troll emerge from the woods.

"You! How did you get up here?"

"Good morrow," he says, panting the words as if he'd been racing to get here. "I have come to see you off."

"It's going to be hard to leave," you say.

"Yes, it is a burdensome pain, but you still have much work to do." He bends at the waist while holding onto his side.

"I'm not sure I'm ready," you say.

"Ready? What an odd word. Must one feel ready to breathe?"

"No. Breathing just happens." You pat his heaving shoulder and smile. "But I'd say that you're having some difficulty finding your own breath!"

The troll replies. "Ha! I'll be fine. I just need to rest a moment."

"But I get what you're saying," you continue. "I don't have to be ready, I just have to be willing."

"And there is the cleverness I saw on the day you chanced by my home."

"Chanced? You mean fell into your trap?"

"Trap or ring of truth?" he asks.

The troll winks as he takes your hand between his leathery fingers and leads you to a flat rock. Tapping the surface, he motions for you to sit down so that you're eye to eye.

"You have traveled a great distance, greater than my satchel would inspire." He smiles enough to expose the gap between his front teeth. "It is as if you flew."

Your eyes light up and you proudly say, "I have solved many mysteries and learned a few tricks as well."

"Ahhh, very good, but I must leave so you can continue along your path, but first…"

"No. Not another riddle!" you interrupt.

"No." he laughs again. "T'is a gift."

"Another present? Really? Do you have more maps?"

The troll squints and cocks his head in confusion. "Maps? You need no more maps. You are here on top of the mountain, you can see in every direction."

"Yes I'm here, but how do I know which is the right way?"

"There is no one to give you a map. You will not find any map in a treasure chest, a satchel or wrapped up as a gift." His eyes grow soft and shiny with the first hint of tears.

"But what path do I take?"

"Choose any, it matters not."

You feel a surge of anger but stop to search for the feeling beneath it. Then the words come, "I feel lost."

The troll uses his sack-cloth sleeve to blow his nose, "Phssshkh." He takes a long inhale, holds up his other sleeve and blows again, "Phssshkh." He drops his arms to his sides and says, "Lost? Now that is a feeling I know. I felt it for the first time the day my mother was taken from me. She was cast with a spell. One moment we were walking together, hand in hand, and the next I found myself wandering the forest alone."

"I'm sorry," you say.

"But I did learn some things. For I too fell into the ring of truth, the deep pit, and that is how I learned to transform my feelings of lost into feelings of love."

He points a clawed finger at some pebbles on the ground and then writes in the air. As if on command, the pebbles take shape and rise. First an "L" appeared, then an "O" and a "V", and finally an "E".

"L - O - V - E?" you spell out loud.

He balls his hand into a fist, then splays his fingers open all at once. More pebbles rise, taking shape to form words beside each letter:

Lose Clinging Own Pain Value Self Enlist Wisdom

"How did you do that?"

"It is time, I must fare thee well." The troll steps closer and wraps his arms around you in a wild hug. You feel his wet sleeves on your neck but sink into the strength of his affection. After a bit he pulls back, placing a hand on each of your shoulders.

Looking deep in your eyes he says, "I give you LOVE. Take it with you on your journey."

He releases his grip and taps your foot with the tip of a soiled boot.

"Go now. Do not tarry. I will not hold you from your journey, nor will I go with you, for your quest is not mine to take. I accept this pain of our parting, for you are my friend."

You want to ask him to reconsider or at least let you follow along. But you listen and heed his message. Your mind knows he's from a different world and it's getting late. Night will soon fall with its dark veil. You have a ways to go before you can rest. You stand and bow to the troll.

"You scared me at first," you say. "But I can see you now. I am grateful for the time we shared."

As you head down into the valley, your heart tells you to be patient and stay open. Things are going to work out. You will choose the right path, one heartbeat at a time.

~

You are not alone during this time of separation. Your story is a singular version of the opener in *A Tale of Two Cities*: "It was the best of times, it was the worst of times… it was the season of Light, it was the season of Darkness, it was the spring of hope, it was the winter of despair..." Your separation may have started in the winter of despair, but like a spring seedling drawn to the sunlight, this is the perfect time to experiment with your new life purpose. Don't stand still. Use the lessons from this book to guide you. Nothing worth having is simple, but the work does get easier when you align your behaviors and your goals with the values of your life.

APPENDIX I: When Grief Becomes Overwhelming

As a psychologist, I was trained not to pathologize grief. Even if a person spends days in bed after a loss, it's best to give them time to heal naturally. Using an earlier version of the psychiatrist's bible for diagnosing mental illness, the *Diagnostic and Statistical Manual of Mental Disorders* (DSM IV), a therapist could not diagnose depression in the first two months of grief. It was as if the manual had erected an impenetrable wall to protect the grieving—but after two months of protection the wall was designed to crumble. This was nonsense. I saw widows referred for therapy because they were still grieving three months after a spouse died. The bereaved would come to their appointment feeling like fugitives of normalcy: "My doctor says I should be over it by now."

Setting a deadline for grief never made anybody feel better. In fact, it adds a layer of fear that "something is wrong" when *nothing* is wrong except for some doctors deciding to throw stones instead of flowers on the coffin.

Is It Grief or Depression?

Thankfully, the DSM V replaced DSM IV and now grief and clinical depression can coexist with one layered over the other. The diagnosis of Major Depressive Disorder is given when sadness keeps the griever from living a productive life, or robs them of their desire to live.

What would you think if you heard a widow say, "I don't want to live without my husband"? You might think it sounds perfectly normal in the first few days of loss. But research has shown that the statement is cause for alarm. It may be a sign of the suicidal thinking that distinguishes "uncomplicated" grief from clinical depression. (Stroebe M, Stroebe W, Abakoumkin G., 2005)

Signs of Clinical Depression

Here are some things to look for to help you decide if your divorce grief has progressed to clinical depression. It may be clinical depression if you have six or more of the following symptoms:

- ☐ You've lost your appetite and over 10% of your weight.
- ☐ You can't get more than three or four hours of sleep most nights.
- ☐ No matter how much sleep you get, you still feel exhausted.
- ☐ The things you used to enjoy give you no pleasure.
- ☐ Even though you're still willing to work on your marriage, you continue to blame yourself for the divorce.
- ☐ Not only do you blame yourself for the loss of your marriage, you're also feeling generally worthless and unlovable.
- ☐ No matter how hard you try, you can't concentrate for long.
- ☐ It feels as though your memory is shot.
- ☐ Sexual activity is either unthinkable or out of control with meaningless partners.
- ☐ Thoughts of suicide emerge and they become more comforting or you think of ways you would do it.

One of the hardest things to do when you're going through a separation is to ask for help. Early on in the grieving process, during the denial and bargaining stages, it's easy to convince yourself that the divorce is not happening or that things will go back to normal: "My marriage isn't over… it can't be." There's a tendency to keep the separation secret in the hopes you'll get back together again. That tendency to keep the secret stops some people from getting help when they need it most. But getting help early is a good thing and it may allow you to get better faster, and *without medication.*

If you can't do it for yourself, do it for the people who count on you to be there. If you think no one needs you, this is the depression talking, your life is valuable. Even if you have zero friends and zero family, there are homeless and needy people who could use your helping hand. Helping others makes the giver feel at least as good as the receiver. Studies show that volunteering helps us to feel more socially connected, and less lonely and depressed.

If you find it too hard to get active and you see yourself in the symptoms of depression above, it may be time to consider medication. But don't expect it to solve all your problems. Do expect, if you're taking the right one, to notice improvement in the physical symptoms of depression.

Medication can help you:

- ✓ Think more clearly
- ✓ Sleep better
- ✓ Feel more energy
- ✓ Regain your appetite

Many people say their thoughts seem less oppressive when they're taking an antidepressant, as if a veil has lifted. There are so many different medicines available today that if one doesn't work, it's likely that another will. The plan is not to stay on an antidepressant forever. However, you should take it for at least six to nine months if it's working. Don't be the person who says, "I felt better so I stopped taking it." That's like saying, "I watered my plant and it grew fine so I stopped watering it." You should not stop taking antidepressant medicine without first talking to your doctor because it can make depression worse, not to mention the preventable side effects.

What Depression Is Not

Depression is not a weakness, nor is it all in your head. Clinical depression is not something you can just "snap out" of like some hypnotic trance. And, it's not like thyroid disease or diabetes, because your doctor can't take a blood test to prove that you're depressed. Since it's psychological, sufferers of depression may feel, or be labeled "lazy" or "weak." They tell themselves they have failed at relationships and perceive it as a failure at life. These beliefs only make it harder to ask for help which can, in turn, worsen the depression. Because depression is associated with a general suppression of the immune system and brain-derived neurotrophic factors (BDNF), a type of growth food for your neurons, this disorder that starts in your brain can result in adverse health effects throughout your entire body.

It's important to keep in mind that what initially causes the depressed mood (say, your breakup) may not be the same as what causes it to persist over time. For example, you may have a family history of depression. This creates a strong hereditary vulnerability to depression, making you more likely to become clinically depressed over your separation. Over time, you might withdraw from friends and family, cut down on doing things you used to enjoy, and feel more hopeless.

There are competing schools of thought regarding the use of antidepressants for grief or depression. I'm a big believer in working through grief naturally and using it to grow stronger… but only to a point. When grief transforms into a clinical depression that becomes disabling, or when worry clouds your ability to get through a day at work or to take care of your responsibilities at home, it's time to consider all your options.

How do you know when it's time to start a medicine or which one is right? This question is best answered by your doctor, since every person's situation is different. Based on the current state of the art in psychiatry, you have about a two-thirds chance of responding positively to the first antidepressant you take. If you're in the one-third that doesn't, don't give up, there are different classes of medicines available.

If you've practiced the principles in this book and still have trouble overcoming your grief, there may be some benefit to seeing a therapist. Keep in mind that many different forms of therapy are available. If ACT doesn't suit you, try another therapy. Our advice is to first try working through your depression with counseling, since it has fewer side effects and can be stopped without physician guidance.

Anxiety Therapy

Anxiety is an unpleasant nervousness including worries about bad things happening in the future. Anxiety is different from fear. Fear is a response to an immediate threat, whereas anxiety is a response to a future, often unrealistic, threat. We all suffer from anxiety from time to time; it's just part of being human. It becomes a disorder when it's chronic and affects your day-to-day life. Many people suffer from anxiety even before they get separated. Some become divorced because their anxiety creates too great a dependency or burden on their marriage. We won't delve into the various types of anxiety conditions here, but I do want to give you a window into how worry can grow from a cute little cub into a full blown tiger.

Case Study: The Worried Rose

When Rose started therapy, she was very worried about her marriage. Her husband, David, had made the move to separate and she was panicked. Rose didn't know how she was going to make ends meet. Affording a mortgage, feeding and clothing the kids— it was all too much for her to juggle.

Rose started telling the children that they would have to give up buying things and going out to eat because she and Daddy were divorcing and they were "poor now." She didn't realize that she was transferring her anxiety about finances onto them. They soon began to act out at school and rebel at home, adding to her distress. When Rose spoke to David about her worries, he complained that he just didn't want to hear it anymore. He'd grown tired of her negativity and her worries about the future.

David agreed to a therapy session for the good of the family, even though he was convinced he would never move back. We learned something important during this session. Rose had a severe anxiety disorder. She was afraid of people and crowds, so she put extra responsibilities on David: "Would you pick up some milk at the supermarket? Oh and some bread, and I need cheese." David explained that once or twice was fine, but Rose would rarely go to the store and never by herself. David would be heading home after a long day at work, slogging through rush hour traffic, looking forward to relaxing and spending time with the family. Then he'd get a call from Rose asking him to head off in a different direction. He felt used and abused.

To make matters worse, Rose refused to go to parties or take trips with her husband, due to her many worries. Because of her limitations, Rose was making repeated withdrawals from the emotional bank account of her marriage without any deposits. When she counter-complained that she did plenty of things for the family, like cooking dinner and keeping a clean house, David let loose his frustration.

"I couldn't care less about those things. In fact, I would love to eat out or pay a cleaning service and forget about the house completely. All that cleaning is just your excuse to stay away from us!"

For the first time in the session, David looked in her eyes and said, "I want a real life—I want my partner by my side, whether it means going shopping, eating at my boss's house, or getting dirty in the park with the kids."

This was a real eye opener for Rose. She thought she was being the perfect wife and mother but instead, her anxiety had driven a wedge into the marriage. David was tired of compensating for her worries. After that session, we knew that Rose had more than relationship work to do. Not only was her anxiety at a peak, she was also depressed. Anxiety and depression tend to go hand in hand. It was clear that she would need a leg up with medication.

David's decision to walk away ultimately saved their marriage. Before their therapy session, she spent most of the time blaming her husband for his callousness: "How could he walk away from his family?" Hearing her husband's side allowed the treatment to be more effective. Once Rose realized that her behavior was based on anxiety and that it was treatable, her husband stopped being her focus in therapy.

With David not in the house and her anxiety finally in check, Rose did her own shopping, joined our divorce group, and went out with her group buddies. She even took a course on medical coding. It took several months, but Rose became more self-sufficient.

Rose's interactions with David changed dramatically as a result of treatment. He saw her doing things for herself, handling the children in new ways, and they were having fun. In David's mind, Rose and fun were like Simon and Garfunkel, they hadn't played together in years. He really did love his family, but his decision to walk away ultimately saved it. Rose did her part; she learned to be okay alone.

Behavioral treatments are the first line of defense for treating anxiety, but some people need anxiety medicine. The best medications are selective serotonin reuptake inhibitors, or SSRIs. They offer "two for one" benefits because they also work on depression. It takes anywhere from two to six weeks for SSRIs to take effect, so patients must take them on faith at the beginning. It's best to avoid sedatives like diazepam, alprazolam, lorazepam, and other drugs known as benzodiazepines because they can worsen depression and cause dependence much like a street drug. Patients like them because they work fast to resolve anxiety but that quick action comes at a cost; they stunt emotional growth and the building of coping skills. The best thing I can compare them to is alcohol. When most people take a shot of alcohol, they feel relaxed. If you ask them to do something that scares them, like give a speech in public, they can do it with that liquid courage. But ask them to give the same speech a day later without the alcohol and they're right back to square one of nervousness. Diazepam, alprazolam, lorazepam, and other benzodiazepines work the same way, by artificially calming your nerves without helping your brain prepare for the long haul.

Here's a list of the most common SSRIs used for treating anxiety:

- ✓ citalopram
- ✓ escitalopram
- ✓ fluoxetine
- ✓ paroxetine
- ✓ sertraline

I treated Rose with fluoxetine starting at 10 mg because this medicine at full strength (20 mg) tends to make people want to jump out of their skin. It's a side effect called "activation," and there is nothing that will make a person bail out of treatment faster. Even at 10 mg, she still felt that it was too much at the beginning, but with encouragement she stuck it out. Within six weeks, her worries had quelled and she felt ready to leave the house.

Obsession Therapy

Obsession is characterized by intrusive thoughts, a persistent attachment to an idea or object, or a preoccupation resistant to any attempts to modify it. Over the course of a single day, you may find yourself thinking often about your ex. It can happen anytime, whether or not it's convenient. This is normal mental activity during a divorce. It doesn't become a disorder unless it's long term and has a serious effect on your well-being. Here are some examples of common behaviors we've seen from people going through a separation.

> *Molly would be sitting in her daily morning meeting at work when the fact that her husband was gone would strike. Her eyes would well up with tears. It would happen at the same point each day—about halfway through her meeting.*
>
> *Chuck would repeatedly see images of his wife with another man and was convinced she was having an affair. He would drive by her house every night to check for an unfamiliar vehicle. He had access to her mobile phone records on their family plan, so he'd reverse check the numbers that came in. When he saw her on the weekend while visiting the kids, he would note what she was wearing.*
>
> *June keyed her husband's car one morning after she stayed up all night outside his empty apartment waiting for him to return. She later discovered from her sister that he'd gone camping with his brother-in-law for the weekend.*

Are any of these behaviors enough to start medication? In and of themselves, they don't necessarily mean these people are suffering from an obsessive disorder. The key is not how irrational the behavior sounds. Believe me, early separation behaviors can seem pretty "out there." The real issue is the impact it has on the obsessive individual's life, for example, if June was so obsessed with her husband's actions that she couldn't:

- ✓ Sleep or eat because of her worries
- ✓ Hold down a job
- ✓ Function as a mom to properly care for her children
- ✓ Spend time with friends or family because of her obsessive worry

Then, yes, it's time to consider medication. There is a word for obsessive worry—"rumination." The term can be used in different ways. For instance, it's used to describe the way a cow chews its food; it chews grass for a time and then swallows. After it swallows, the cud comes back up, and the cow chews it again. This process repeats over and over again, just like the thoughts that sometimes arise during a separation.

We often think about our ex: how they hurt us, how they left us, why they left, whether they are ever coming back. Then we force ourselves to stop, get back to work, and let it go. We can do this for a time and then the thought comes back and, just like the cow, we chew on it all over again. We ruminate naturally—it's not a conscious act. Ruminating mixed with a depressed mood and the inability to function for extended periods may be a sign that it's time to consider psychotherapy.

Some common behaviors that alone might not be a big problem, can spell trouble when they occur together. These include:

- ✓ Inability to stop talking about your ex despite repeated attempts
- ✓ Continuing to call or leaving voicemails, texts, or instant messages despite being told to stop
- ✓ Repeated unwelcomed, unannounced visits
- ✓ Raging or uncontrolled reactions
- ✓ Inability to experience even brief moments of happiness
- ✓ Using your children as a sounding board for your complaints about your ex

Other serious signs of obsessional reactions to grief are stalking or making threats of violence to control the escaping spouse.

Behavioral therapy, and sometimes SSRIs, are helpful for obsessional disorders as long as they have not become delusional. A delusion is a fixed, false belief. An example of a delusional obsession would be thinking that your ex has infected you with HIV despite several blood studies and doctors' opinions that you're not showing any evidence of being infected.

Many people will balk at the suggestion that medicine should be used as a treatment during a separation, but when used correctly, I've seen it lift people from the pits of hopelessness to a functioning, hopeful life. People who could barely muster the energy to get out of bed in the morning get back to work, feeling better and more in control. If you're wondering whether you need medicine, understand that it's important to try psychotherapy first. Skipping this vital step may prolong the time it takes to achieve your long-term goals.

APPENDIX II: Resources

Resources for those suffering from abuse:

http://www.ncjfcj.org/resource-library/publications/managing-your-divorce-guide-battered-women

http://www.uscis.gov/humanitarian/battered-spouse-children-parents

http://www.thehotline.org

References

Aesop. (2007). The Wolf and the Lamb. In D.L. Ashliman (Ed.), Aesop's Fables (pp. 102-116). New York: Penguin Group Bond, F. W., & Bunce, D. (2000). Mediators of change in emotion-focused and problem-focused worksite stress management interventions. Journal of Occupational Health Psychology, 5, 156-163.

Brach, T. (2004). Radical acceptance: embracing your life with the heart of a Buddha. New York: Bantam Books.

Branstetter, A. D., Wilson, K. G., Hildebrandt, M., & Mutch, D. (2004). Improving psychological adjustment among cancer patients: ACT and CBT. Paper presented at the Association for Advancement of Behavior Therapy, New Orleans.

Buber, M., & Kaufmann, W. A. (1996). I and thou: Martin Buber; a new translation with a prologue "I and You" and notes. New York, NY: Simon & Schuster.

McCarthy, C. (2007). No country for old men. New York: Vintage Books.

Dahl, J., Wilson, K. G., & Nilsson, A. (2004). Acceptance and Commitment Therapy and the treatment of persons at risk for long-term disability resulting from stress and pain symptoms: A preliminary randomized trial. Behavior Therapy, 35, 785-802.

Diagnostic and statistical manual of mental disorders: DSM-5. (2013). Washington, Londres: American Psychiatric Association.

Erectile Dysfunction Drugs Market Size Will Be Worth $3.2 Billion By 2022: Grand View Research, Inc. (n.d.). Retrieved from https://globenewswire.com/news-release/2015/11/23/789503/0/en/Erectile-Dysfunction-Drugs-Market-Size-Will-Be-Worth-3-2-Billion-By-2022-Grand-View-Research-Inc.html

Gibran, K. (1924). The Prophet by Kahlil Gibran. New York: A.A. Knopf.

Harris, R. (2006). Embracing your demons: An overview of acceptance and commitment therapy. Psychotherapy in Australia, 12(4), 2-8

Hayes, S. C., Strosahl, K. D., & Wilson, K. G. (2016). Acceptance and commitment therapy: the process and practice of mindful change. New York: Guilford Press.

Hayes, S. C. (2004). Acceptance and commitment therapy, relational frame theory, and the third wave of behaviour therapy. Behaviour Therapy, 35, 639–665.

Kabat-Zinn, J. (2013). Full catastrophe living: using the wisdom of your body and mind to face stress, pain, and illness. New York: Bantam Books Trade Paperbacks.

Kevin C. Paul, Private Property: A Discourse on Gender Inequality in American Law, 7 Law & Ineq. 399 (1989).

Kübler-Ross, E. (1974). Questions and answers on death and dying. New York: Macmillan.

Locker, Lawrence, William D. McIntosh, Amy Hackney, Janie H. Wilson, Katherine E. Wiegand (2010). "The Breakup of Romantic Relationships: Situational Predictors of Perception of Recovery." North American Journal of Psychology, 12 (3): 565-578.

Levant, R. F. (2001). Desperately seeking language: Understanding, assessing and treating normative male alexithymia. In G. R. Brooks and G. Good (Eds). The new handbook of counseling and psychotherapy for men. (Vol. 1, pp. 424-443). San Francisco: Jossey-Bass.

Linehan, M. (1993). Cognitive-behavioral treatment of borderline personality disorder. New York: Guilford Press.

Siever, L. J. (2008). The Neurobiology of Aggression and Violence. American Journal of Psychiatry, 165(4), 229-242.

Stroebe, M., Stroebe, W., Schoot, R. V., Schut, H., Abakoumkin, G., & Li, J. (2014). Guilt in Bereavement: The Role of Self-Blame and Regret in Coping with Loss. PLoS ONE, 9(5). doi:10.1371/journal.pone.0096606

Tannen, D. (2001). You Just Don't Understand: Women and Men in Conversation. Milsons Point, NSW: Random House.

Twohig, M. P., Hayes, S. C., & Masuda, A. (2006). Increasing Willingness to Experience Obsessions: Acceptance and Commitment Therapy as a Treatment for Obsessive-Compulsive Disorder. Behavior Therapy, 37(1), 3-13.

Frankl, V. E. (2006). Man's Search for Meaning. Boston: Beacon Press.

Vlemincx, E., Diest, I. V., & Bergh, O. V. (2016). A sigh of relief or a sigh to relieve: The psychological and physiological relief effect of deep breaths. Physiology & Behavior, 165, 127-135. doi:10.1016/j.physbeh.2016.07.004

Wegner, D. M., Schneider, D. J., Carter, S. R., & White, T. L. (1987). Paradoxical effects of thoughts suppression. Journal of Personality and Social Psychology, 53, 5–13.

Zettle, R. D., & Rains, J. C. (1989). Group cognitive and contextual therapies in treatment of depression. Journal of Clinical Psychology, 45, 438-445.

Made in the USA
Coppell, TX
07 July 2023

18848711R00140